BEYOND EVACUATION

ANN'S WORLD'S END

BY

DEIRDRE ANN YARDLEY

For all my friends both at home and abroad,
and especially those in the 'Walking for Health' group.

BEYOND EVACUATION
Ann's Worlds End

INTRODUCTION

My first book, "Ann's Evacuation Country Style", was published by Amazon in 2016. In it I tell the story of my evacuation in September, 1939, at the age of six.

The feedback from the book has been most enjoyable. From an elderly family friend came the comment on "the winsome little face" looking at her from the cover – language not often used these days. Many people have commented that it brought back memories of their own childhood, or war years, and how enjoyable – mostly – that was. The most frequent questions I have been asked were "What happened next?" and "When do we get the next part?" which prompted me to begin this continuation.

Here I describe how I return from evacuation in the countryside during the early part of the war to a very different way of life in town during the latter stages of the war.

CHAPTERS

CHAPTER I
Returning Home

Born a city child, early in the war I had been sent for safety to live with a family in the country. Unlike many of my fellow evacuees who suffered pangs of homesickness, I had taken to country life like a duck to water. My enthusiasm was evidently catching, as sometime later my mother and small sister had joined me there and this lovely cottage in a cherry orchard had become our home.

It was still war time in 1943 and I was ten years old. The last four years had been spent in the country, living in the cottage which was built around 1470, and which is now classed as a Grade II listed building.

Aston Bank Cottage, Elizabeth centre, Ann on right

Now, however, everything was set to change. Mr. Moore, the farmer at Aston Bank Farm who owned the cottage in which we lived, had died. His farm was sold and the new owner wanted our cottage for his agricultural worker, so we had to leave. It was 1943, still wartime, and I was ten years old. My country life was over.

Mother, my sister Elizabeth and I now returned to our old home which we had left at the beginning of the war.

Our home in Birmingham

Our home was a semi-detached house on the outskirts of Birmingham that was built in 1934. This was vastly different living from our last four years because we now had electricity, electric lights instead of paraffin lamps, taps which ran cold water instead of a pump, and even hot water after the emersion heater had been switched on by a lever attached to a box on the landing. We had a bathroom with a bath and could turn on the tap from which ran hot water. Oh joy! Actually we were supposed to have no more than five inches of water in the bath and everyone took turns, Elizabeth went first, I was next in the bath, Mother followed and Father came last. Water had to be conserved in case it was needed for fire fighting. Nevertheless there was no more sitting in a tin bath in front of the range and filling it with water from the kettle. No more pumping ice-cold water into a bowl in which I stood in the little scullery for a stand-up all-over wash.

Upstairs, as well as the bathroom, there was a separate lavatory – oh yes, no more using the chamber pot kept under the bed, nor running out of the door, half way round the cottage, through the outhouse to the lavatory with a wooden seat and a bucket underneath. I believe Father emptied it each weekend when he came to see us, into a pit at the back of the garden.

Here there were three bedrooms leading off a landing. Mother and Father had the large front room where Elizabeth had been with them when she was so ill during her first years. Elizabeth was now six years old. She and I shared the large back bedroom overlooking the garden and there was a smaller front bedroom. Grandfather Adams, Mother's father, lived with us for a time and this was his room.

We children had to keep our bedroom clean and tidy and I distinctly remember keeping my side immaculate while pushing all the dust over onto Elizabeth's side. There were no fitted carpets for us in those days. Upstairs we had lino floor covering. It was the fore-runner of today's cushion flooring tiles.

Downstairs there were two rooms – reception rooms they were called. The front one facing south and therefore the sunny one, was being used as the sitting room (we called it the lounge) and the back room facing north and always sunless, we used as the dining room. In these reception rooms the floors were covered with a large square carpet, leaving wood surrounds which were kept polished. The kitchen was alongside the dining room at the end of the hall. The hall had oak parquet floor tiles which always shone as Mother spent hours on her knees polishing this floor with beeswax polish. It was her pride and joy.

In the kitchen we now had a free-standing cooker, a gas cooker with the maker's name, New World. It was definitely "New World" after our trials and tribulations with the calor-gas rings Mother had cooked on in the cottage. The flooring here was red quarry tiles, oh so cold if one stood on them barefoot.

Just off the kitchen with a door from the hall was the pantry where large crockery, saucepans, kitchen utensils and sundries were kept. Food was put on the shelves, vegetables in a rack and milk in bottles stood on the floor. We had no refrigerator to keep food cool. In hot weather milk bottles were stood in a bucket of cold water to prevent the milk turning sour. In here were also kept biscuit and cake tins which Mother always seemed able to fill. Early each morning I would be first up and they would hear me rattling the tins looking for something to appease my hunger. As Mother said, I always had hollow legs!

Outside the kitchen door was the garage and the coal house and right outside was the outside lavatory or toilet. Two toilets! Weren't we lucky! These toilets had a cistern, which was the water tank at the top of the wall. It had a lever with a long chain which, when pulled, flushed the toilet. A real flush! What a luxury!

In the garage was a wall cupboard where Father kept his small tools and bottles, jars and tins in which he hoarded nails, screws, washers and anything which might come in useful. I was fascinated with the contents of this cupboard and maybe that is why, when I was about six, I had felt I had to write my name on the outside of the door. One writes normally across the page from left to right but, as I am left-handed, it felt normal for me to write from the right to the left, BACKWARDS!

There must be something wrong with my brain! I was taken to the doctor's for investigation. I was declared quite sane! And there my name remained, written backwards on that cupboard door for all to see.

I mentioned the coalhouse. Each reception room and the kitchen had a coal fire. There was no central heating here. The grates had to be cleared of ash each morning before the fire could be laid for the day. We had a gas poker which was attached to a small gas tap beside the fireplace. The poker would be placed in the grate then small bits of wood and small pieces of coal would be placed on top. The gas would be turned on, a lighted match thrown onto the coal and the gas would ignite with a loud "pop". Then the fire would begin to burn and the poker would be removed. Occasionally the fire would die and Mother would quickly get a sheet of newspaper and hold it up in front of the fire to make it 'draw' causing a draught to go up the chimney and encouraging the flames to pick up and start the fire going again. Sometimes the fire would flare up very well very quickly and as it got hotter the newspaper Mother was holding would scorch. Before it could set on fire it was very quickly taken away and screwed up. There was no thought of "health and safety" in those days. When we sat before the warm fire our legs would get heated at the front but our backs would still be cold.

We had the coal delivered by the coalman who, after a hundredweight had been ordered, would arrive in his flat-bed truck with full coal sacks stacked upright in rows. The sacks were large, very strong, Hessian-style bags with two handles, one on each side of the top of the sack. The coal man, wearing his jacket with leather- covered shoulders and back, would stand at the side of the truck and drag a bag to the edge where, with his back to it he would grab the handles to hoist it on to his back. Moving as fast as he could under the weight he would then stagger round to the coalhouse and with a jerk of his bottom tip out the coal over his head into the coalhouse. Mother would ask me to stand inside the kitchen door and count the number of bags he emptied, just to make sure we were not short-changed.

The weight tables we learnt at school and recited were:-

16 ounces (ozs.) = 1 pound (lb.)
14 pounds (lbs.) = 1 stone (st.)
2 stones (sts.) = 1 quarter (qur.)
4 quarters (qurs.) = 1 hundredweight (cwt.)

The coalman delivered eight sacks of coal, so I guess one sack of coal weighed one stone. No metric measures for us! If the coal lumps shone or glistened it was good coal and burned well, but if it was dull it would not burn at all well.

Every fireplace had a chimney so every house would have chimneys on the roof. Coal fires made smoke which produced soot in the chimney and if this was not scraped or brushed out every so often it would set fire to the chimney and flames would come out of it above the roof. When this happened to us, before long a group of by-standers gathered outside watching while inside we threw salt on the fire to douse the flames and waited to see if the flames outside subsided. Oh! The acrid smell was everywhere. Fortunately for us the chimney fire did not flame long enough to send for the fire brigade.

Father was our chimney sweep. He had his own set of brush and rods. First he would drop a sheet from the mantelpiece over the front of the fireplace, then put another sheet on the floor in front. He would screw a rod into the flat, circular, stiff brush and place this under the sheet and up the chimney, adding another rod which he screwed in as he pushed it upwards. There was a limited amount of flexibility in the rods, allowing them to be bent slightly to push round from below and up the chimney, and the sheet was clutched tightly round the rod so that no soot could escape. This he continued to do until there were no more rods left. I now made it my important job to go outside to see if I could see the brush appearing out of the top of the chimney. An excited "YES" brought me running in, after which Father pulled on the rods to bring the brush down along with all the soot which had collected in the chimney. He had to be so careful not to allow any soot to escape into the room.

Chimney Sweep

12

What a dirty, filthy mess it made although the sheets had prevented it falling into the room. The soot had to be shovelled into a bucket and taken out to the garden where it could be spread around to help fertilise the soil. It was then Mother's job to clear up the fireplace with a cloth and a bucket of hot, soapy water. Soot clung to everything.

CHAPTER II
Worlds End Road

We lived in Handsworth Wood, a district on the northern boundary of Birmingham, about three-and-a-half miles from the city centre.

The plot of land on which our house was built was wider than the others in the road. We were at the end of the road, the last house but one. This wider strip at the side of the garage was where the Anderson shelter was housed behind the fence. It was here that my parents and our neighbours would go when the air-raid warnings sounded.

It was built by Father from sheets of corrugated iron standing deep in the ground and forming an arched roof overhead. The whole was covered with turf, making it invisible from above. Three steps down from the path at the side of the garage took us into the dark, dank interior of the shelter, with a bench to seat about six on either side, and here the occupants would sit and wait, until the "All Clear" sounded, praying meanwhile that no bombs would be dropped from overhead. A candle would be lit to give a little light to lift the gloom. A tarpaulin was hung over the entrance which could be dropped down when all were inside so that no light could be seen. Biscuits and a hot drink from a flask would be offered if anyone had thought to bring them. I was very fortunate to experience this only once, on a week-end visit back from the country.

The Anderson shelter was built side-on to the garden, its front entrance facing the garage. In the space, along the shelter's side, Father had built us a sand pit and a swing. The sand pit was a concrete rectangle with a flat concrete border to walk and sit on. It had a drain hole in one corner at the bottom. On his journeys Father would surreptitiously stop at a beach and fill a bag with sand to put in our sand pit.

The swing was a tall, very high, substantial wooden structure, the base cemented into the ground. It seemed at least twelve feet tall to us though I suppose it was really about eight feet high. We all referred to it as "The Gallows!

Ann, aged 15, on the swing with young cousin Rosemarie

The wooden seat had four holes through which very long, strong, thick, ropes were passed, each ending with a turkshead knot. Father was very pleased with these knots he had constructed. I could sit on this swing and pump my legs backwards and forwards to gain a great height enabling me to see over the fence at the front and way away down the garden at the back to the houses in the distance at the bottom of the garden. It was my aim to go higher and higher until the ropes were almost horizontal, then they would relax, giving a slight jerk before the swing came down on the backward stroke, only to have me pump up again to try to reach an even greater height. I scared Mother stiff!

Forwards and Backwards

Our house was newly built adjoining the farm land of Cherry Orchard Farm, and the road leading down from us was Cherry Orchard Road. How strange that we had spent the early part of the war in a 15th century cottage in the middle of a cherry orchard. Our road was appropriately called Worlds End Road.

From the height of the swing I could see over the gardens, ours and those of the houses built at the bottom of our garden, over the road in front of those houses to a row of small shops.

The Garden

16

There was a green-grocer's at the end of this row of shops. Mrs. Collar came next with her draper's shop where she sold some baby wear, ladies' underwear and haberdashery. I was always fascinated to see Mrs. Collar walk as she had very flat feet which always flapped as she walked, like those of clowns in the circus. There was Mr. Watts with the newsagent's and post office. The lino covering his floor was so very worn. He sold sweets but we rarely bought any at that time, as sweets were rationed and could only be bought with coupons in our ration books. The hardware shop came next, then the chemist. Ah! The chemist sold Horlicks tablets for making drinks but they were a good enough substitute for sweets so we spent our pocket money on those. Victory V throat or cough sweets were another substitute, tasting of aniseed. If I remember rightly, there was a butcher and Mr. Rawle the grocer. This row of little shops supplied all our needs. On the pavement outside Mr. Watts' was the red telephone box and a pillar box, commonly called a post box. This brings to mind the marvellous service provided by the Royal Mail. The first delivery of the day came around seven o'clock in the morning and there was a second delivery at eleven o'clock each day.

There were other daily deliveries. The milkman called early every day and at the end of the week on a Friday he would call to collect the money. My mother had joined the Co-operative Society and was allocated a number, so each week when she paid the milkman he would write her number beside the payment on a tear-off strip in his book and give this receipt to Mother to impale on a spike to keep as a record while the carbon copy remained in his book. For years I remember giving this number, 233359. Then every so often I would accompany Mother to the head office where she would collect her dividend which helped along the family finances.

The baker from Roy's Bakery came round too in his horse and cart which resembled an open caravan. It had lantern lights at each side. As darkness descended the lights were lit to warn other road users of its presence. The baker would descend from his cart, a large basket on his arm, to deliver the loaves of bread.

17

Every so often the rag and bone man would come round the roads with his horse-drawn flat-bed cart. The horse's nosebags full of hay and oats and a bucket containing water would be swinging from the back as he called out for "Any Old Iron". He would take away anything we wanted to get rid of.

Occasionally the scissor grinder man would come round on his bike and knock on the doors asking if we wanted any scissors, knives or shears sharpened. We declined as Father always did any sharpening we needed.

The activity which gave us children most delight came in the hottest part of the year when it was deemed time to repair the road. A machine would spread the sticky black tar over the road and the huge steam roller would come pounding down the road with the controller rapidly turning his wheel this way and that so that the huge front roller would flatten all the hot tar. We children would run on the pavement alongside, backwards and forwards to keep up with this gigantic puffing machine. It had to be done in hot weather because the tar was then at its most malleable but, oh dear, how it stuck to our shoes if we trod anywhere near. Woe betide us if we took any into the house on to the carpet. This road mending was an annual occurrence which was enjoyed by us children, including the hot, tarry smell. The smell of the tar was believed to be beneficial for children with asthma.

CHAPTER III
Perry Hall Park

Opposite the front of our house was the bluebell wood, a wonderful place to play. It was here that, years before, my little Scottie dog, Sally, had gone to investigate a noise. At that time there was very little traffic on the roads, especially near to us, but I had heard a car engine approaching from Cherry Orchard Road and had called to Sally to stay there. She had misinterpreted my call and had come running back to me, only to be run over. I was a very sad six year old.

From the end of the road, a step away from our house, was a lane leading down to the railway and over the railway bridge into the playing fields, or park as we called it. During this wartime, ack-ack guns were stationed there standing on top of the players' changing rooms or pavilion. They were often heard shooting away at night when enemy planes were around. The search lights would light up the sky, criss-crossing over each other. One large, grey barrage balloon sailed over the playing fields close to the railway line, anchored by strong wires to keep it from sailing away. The barrage balloons were supposedly to keep enemy planes from flying too low. There were army Nissan huts in the park under the Scots pine trees beside the railway line too, which were used by the army personnel. It was not until after the war had ended that all was demolished and the park returned to playing fields where football matches were played once again.

This land, now the park, had once been the estate belonging to a large house, Perry Hall. Before the war there had been tall iron gates at the entrances to the park which were closed and locked each night by the park keeper to keep people out. The park keeper was in the park during the daytime keeping everyone in order. Should we attempt to ride our bikes around or through the park we were soon told off if he saw us. If we espied him first we would quickly dismount and looking innocent would push our bikes past him until he was out of sight. Then we would jump back onto our bikes and pedal away as fast as we could.

I loved riding my bike around the park along the paths and over the three wooden bridges which crossed the fast flowing River Tame. This ran through the park making it a dangerous place to play. I was very law abiding when "the parky" was in view. I once chose to ride my bike across the grass and was going quite fast when the front wheel hit a rut and over the handlebars I went, not badly hurt, but, of course, I could not admit it as I should not have been riding anyway.

In this part of the park, across the wooden bridges, was another attraction. There was a man-made boating pool like a moat around a centre where Perry Hall once stood. Over this moat were two concrete bridges inviting me to pedal hard up them on my bike and whiz down the other side. Beneath these were the paddle boats. Occasionally I was given some money to have a go on a paddle boat and it was great fun to paddle all round the pool under the concrete bridges trying hard to avoid bumping into them or into any other boat which was having difficulty steering a sraight course. Turning the right-hand handle turned the right-hand paddle which spun the boat to the left! Turning the left-hand handle turned the left-hand paddle which spun the boat to the right! Turning both together should have sent the boat on a straight course forward. Of course, if I turned the handles backwards, all this paddling was reversed. Woe betide any other boat which tried to avoid us or bump into us. How fast we could go depended on how fast I could turn the handles, until my arms ached.

Paddle Boat

Sometimes I took my young sister, Elizabeth, with me with strict instructions to mind what I was doing and take care not to fall in. I must look after Elizabeth. She was not old enough or strong enough to turn the handles which turned the paddles to move the boat. Occasionally she would want to have a go at turning the handles and it was a wonder we were not tipped into the water as we exchanged places, rocking the boat in the process. The switch over did not last long. The boat rocked perilously again as we resumed our original seats, out of view of the boatman of course. Our sixpence a turn was soon used up and the boatman would call in our boat number. He kept a strict eye on the paddlers. There was no sneaking an extra paddle round the pool.

At the far end of this park was a pool where we could spend hours with a fishing net trying to catch sticklebacks to put into our jam jars. At this side of the park there were also tall iron railings and gates which were locked by the park keeper each night at sunset but during the war they were removed for use in making further armaments. After the war ended, park keepers were no longer employed though the no cycling rule still applied.

What freedom we children had in those days.

CHAPTER IV
Primary School

Turning from the house in the opposite direction to the lane leading down to the park was the way to school, along Butlers Road. Each morning and each late afternoon two girls, one aged ten, the other six years old, could be seen walking along this road intent on reaching their approaching assault course. At the bottom of the very long garden belonging to a large Victorian house which was on the main road and bus route into Birmingham, there were tall, black iron railings and through these railings grew huge, thick plant stems with gigantic leaves which hung over the pavement. Here we jumped over them, high and low, always trying to improve our performance. We did not know then that these plants were the scourge of the country, imported by Victorians to decorate their gardens. Japanese knotweed, once introduced, is very difficult to eradicate. These stems were our obstacle course.

Further on, as the road turned the corner into Wood Lane, we enjoyed another variation on our walk. Modern houses had been built and each had a run up over the pavement from the road to their driveway. There was a tall hawthorn hedge in front of the houses and between this and the front gardens was a well-used track – well-used by children that is – who always chose to run behind the hedge, up and down as the track rose and fell either side of the driveways. It was a marvellous running track as we kept appearing and disappearing from view, right up to the main road. As our school lunchtime was from 12 noon until 2.00 p.m. I always came home for dinner and had plenty of time to enjoy myself here.

Elizabeth attended a school on Marsh Hill at Stockland Green. To get there involved a bus journey on the Outer Circle bus route which went all round the outskirts of Birmingham. There were two circular bus routes in Birmingham. The Outer Circle, number 11, went all round the outer-lying districts of Birmingham and a good afternoon could be spent riding on a bus all round the Outer Circle route with plenty to see from the front seat upstairs. There were many semi-detached houses with gardens, built just before the war, and plenty of greenery.

The Inner Circle bus route, number 8, went round the industrial districts closer to the city centre where factories large and small were to be found, such as the little workshops in the jewellery quarter or the larger factories like "HP Sauce" at Aston Cross and "Ansell's Brewery" at Cape Hill. The smell of their ingredients permeated the air. Here the houses were of a much earlier construction, many of the old back-to-back variety which were built around a yard which housed the communal toilet and washhouse. It was in the inner city area that the results of the war were more evident as factory areas had been targeted and bombed.

Each schoolday morning Elizabeth and I would arrive at the bus stop for   8.25 a.m. At this bus stop was a free standing clock for the drivers of the Outer Circle buses to key in the time of their arrival and departure. Sometimes an inspector would be standing there as inspectors were very frequently on the buses checking the tickets, the stages where passengers had boarded the bus and that they had paid the correct fare. All buses had a conductor or conductress. These would be smartly dressed in a navy blue uniform and would have a leather satchel for the money slung over one shoulder and a metal punching machine slung over the other. They carried a rack of tickets, one of which they punched at the appropriate stage on the side of the ticket for the passenger when he paid his money. The bus drivers were always smartly dressed in their navy uniform, white shirt and black tie and always wore a peaked cap.

Elizabeth would get on the Outer Circle bus at 8.25 a.m. and sit on the long seat just inside. The conductor would see that she left the bus at the correct stop opposite her school at Stockland Green. She had green tokens to give up for her fare which had been acquired by Mother from the Council offices. Elizabeth arrived back at the Outer Circle bus stop in the afternoon at about 4.30 p.m. and sometimes I would be waiting there to meet her. Invariably she would have a lump of cheese in her pocket, presumably for sustenance on the way home.

I would leave her in the morning to continue my walk to school along the main road to Birmingham. I went past the pub and small hotel called The Endwood, and over the branch line railway to Great Barr, past the blacksmith's forge and the rectory to the corner shop owned by Mr. Spalding where I turned left down church Hill Road to school. It was 1943 and still wartime. I had returned from evacuation to my old school, Saint Mary's Church of England Primary School. This old Victorian school had tall, narrow windows built specially so that children could not see out and be distracted from their lessons. As in many such small schools, the large classroom was divided by a wooden partition with glass windows and it could be pushed back on runners to make one large classroom or drawn closed to make two classrooms, one for the infants and one for the juniors. There was a further classroom for the top juniors on the other side of the school entrance. Here, there was a cloakroom which opened into a small square entrance hall leading to the Head Mistress' room in the corner. This entrance and cloakroom were the boys' and outside was a wide strip of grass where they could play, as well as the normal playground surrounding the school. The girls' cloakroom and playground were on the other side of the school with outside toilets at the bottom. A wall divided the boys' playground from the girls'. It was here that I was asked to twizzle in my grey skirt which ballooned like an umbrella. I twizzled till it rose higher and higher. I was delighted with it. So were the boys looking over the wall.

Twizzling

The first girl I spoke to on my first morning back at the school was Margaret, a pretty girl with black curly hair and who,

24

from that day, has remained my life-long friend. I was a plain child with my hair scraped back and plaited. We were both in the same class with Mr. George, our teacher. He liked pretty girls! They were favourites.

Our desks for two were the sort that had a tip-up seat with a back rest. Each side had a desk lid and along the top of the desk was a groove to hold our pens and pencils. On the right hand side, above the groove, each desk had a hole into which an inkwell was dropped. Monitors brought round freshly filled inkwells each morning. Our penholders were wooden, onto which had been pushed a metal bracket into which a nib was inserted. This pen had to be continually dipped into the inkwell when writing and consequently the ink did not only stay on the nib. Fingers became ink stained, the pristine wooden penholder would become inked all over, blots of ink would appear on our written pages and blotting paper would be much in evidence. All we were given was just a small square of blotting paper torn from a larger sheet. There was a war on, paper was in short supply. This was economy!

Our desks were arranged in rows, all facing the front. I preferred to sit at the front of the class and I remember one morning when Mr. George was asking the class questions I turned round to see the girl, Anne, at the back of the class giving an answer. The next thing I knew was a clip on the back of my head and Mr. George, the teacher, saying, in no uncertain terms, "Don't tell her the answer." It was the last thing I intended doing. I was mortified.

I remember a painting lesson we had one afternoon. We took our own paint boxes to school. These were metal boxes with small cubes of paint in a row and space below to hold a paint brush. We dipped the brush in water then scrubbed it on the desired cube of paint. There was a jam jar of bluebells on Mr. George's desk and these flowers were distributed among our desks. As I painted mine, having no idea of mixing colours to provide the right shade, Mr. George came round, stood over me, and, poking his finger at my painting, said scornfully "Do you really think the green stem is that colour?" I shrank in my seat. I do not think I was a popular pupil.

25

One morning each week the boys were taken to the swimming baths for their swimming lesson under Mr. George's care and eagle eye, and while they were away a girl from the class was chosen to sit at his desk on a dais at the front of the class to keep order. I was chosen one week and all went well. When it came to the next week I was called out again to sit at the teacher's desk. "But Mr. George, I did it last week. It is somebody else's turn." I was not being rude, just fair as I thought. I was told, "You will do it again." Perhaps I was very good at keeping order. But years later it occurred to me that any girl whose name I had written down for misbehaving would be hauled over the coals by Mr. George when he returned. Not a very pleasant thought. No-one misbehaved.

On four mornings a week we all went into one classroom for our morning assembly. My friend, Margaret, could play the piano and I remember her sitting primly on the chair in front of the piano, arms raised slightly in order to reach the keys, and playing "The March of the Tin Soldiers" as we marched out in time and back to our classrooms. But every Wednesday morning, as it was a church school, we would walk, in crocodile fashion, from the school to St. Mary's Church at the top of the road for a short service taken by the curate. We learnt the ten commandments which I still think is an excellent set of rules for leading a good life.

When we returned we looked forward to our one third of a pint of milk (1/3 pt.) which all school children had each morning. Milk monitors brought into the classroom the crates of little milk bottles which had circular cardboard tops each with a circular centre bit which we pushed down and into the hole inserted a straw for drinking. When the milk was drunk we went out to play. In the afternoons we had craft lessons. We made mats using the cardboard milk bottle tops which we had saved, wrapping them round, through the central hole, using raffia in different colours. Several finished ones would be joined together to make a larger mat – gifts for our mothers.

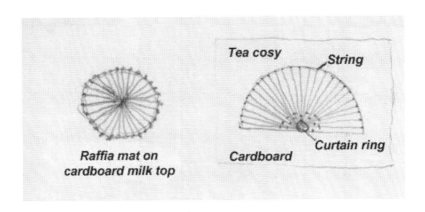

Tea cosy
String
Curtain ring
Cardboard

Raffia mat on
cardboard milk top

I progressed to making a tea cosy using brown and yellow wool. On a large piece of cardboard a semicircle was drawn and on this semicircle holes would be pierced at a half inch distance from each other. Along the straight bottom at the halfway position a curtain ring was fixed on each side of the cardboard. String would be threaded through each hole on the semicircle and through the curtain ring alternately on each side of the cardboard until a fan shape was achieved on both sides. Then weaving began from the centre curtain ring until the shape was filled on one side at a time, using different colours to make the pattern. When all the weaving was done the cardboard was torn away leaving the completed tea cosy.

It was still wartime. The Government brought in a scheme for saving money. At home, each week, Mrs. Hollins would call, for Mother to buy National Savings stamps. These stamps were stuck on a card and when it was filled up the card was exchanged for a savings certificate. Schools were encouraged to adopt this scheme and every Monday morning the teacher would sell these stamps which we would buy at sixpence each to stick on our card. Likewise our cards would be exchanged for our savings certificates when they were filled up.

Another savings idea was to have a sum of money to aim at. A large poster was secured to the front of the classroom wall with a chart marking off the amounts up to fifty pounds (£50). To us children it was a huge sum in those days. We were astounded when, next morning, David Collar, son of Mrs. Collar in the haberdasher's shop in the road behind our house, brought a cheque from his father for this whole amount. We all clapped long and loud. Of course we then had to change our target.

The time came for Mr. George to retire but before leaving he had all his class out on the grass in the boys' playground in order to take photographs, especially one of the prettiest girls.

I enjoyed school life on the whole, more so when we had a new teacher. But one morning will remain for ever in my memory. As usual, I walked with Elizabeth to the Outer Circle bus stop but this morning she said she did not want to go to school and would not get on the bus. What should I do? With just my pocket money in my pocket I quickly decided I would have to go on the bus with her to Stockland Green. When we reached her bus stop I saw her safely off to school then caught the next bus back to our starting point and hurried off down to my school. It was Tuesday morning. As I approached the school building I heard singing. It had slipped my mind that it was hymn practice morning which was taken by the head mistress, Miss Chandler. I was ten minutes late. Miss Chandler announced that everyone who was late would miss their playtime and report to her. I was in tears. I explained that Elizabeth, my sister, did not want to go to school so I took her on the bus to her school at Stockland Green but Miss Chandler did not, or would not, believe me. I was late so I would miss my playtime. And miss my playtime I did! How unfair was it? It rankled with me for years afterwards.

The way home from school took us past the corner shop at the top of Church Hill Road. It was owned by Mr. Spalding. I do remember, when I was several years younger before the war, buying a long golden twisted stick of barley sugar which Mrs. Spalding took out of the large glass jar with the screw top which stood on the shelf behind the counter. After untwisting the cellophane paper surrounding the barley sugar there was nothing better than sucking the sugary stick all the way home, juice running out of my mouth onto my sticky fingers.

Another sweet I remember of those days was Cadbury's halfpenny (½d) bars of chocolate. Grandmother Adams bought me six of these small bars which were about four inches long and an inch wide, flat underneath and rounded on top with the Cadbury's logo etched on top. They were put in a white triangular paper bag. How I loved to suck these bars to a point all the way down to the end. These memories must have been before the war, before sweet rationing was brought in, before my evacuation when I would have been about six year old. In 1943 we still had sweet rationing.

Leaving the corner shop we went up the main road which at that time saw very few vehicles. We passed the rectory and came to a very small terrace of old houses end on to the road and up a slight rise. At the beginning of this terrace was the blacksmith's forge which had a stable door, the top half being open while the bottom half remained closed. If we heard the blacksmith hammering we would rush up to look over the closed half of the door hoping to see the horse patiently waiting while the blacksmith, standing before his furnace, was hammering away making the new horse shoes. We were very disappointed to find the shed all shut up on those days when the blacksmith was not working.

St. Mary's C of E School		Handsworth.	
Childs Name	Ann Yardley		
Subject	Marks Maximum	Marks Obtained	Place in Class
Arithmetic Mental	20	9	7th out of 24
Arithmetic Written	100	66	
English	110	104	
Reading	10	10	
Writing	10	10	
Attendance	good		
Conduct	Excellent a pleasure to teach		

Primary School Report on Leaving

29

The time was approaching to leave the primary school. Most of us in the top juniors sat the scholarship or 11-plus as it became known. We girls went to the Grammar School to take the exam. On the day the postman brought the result I remember Mother saying I had not passed for the High School as they had expected but I had obtained a place at King Edward's Grammar School for girls, Handsworth. I think I must have been nervous when faced with exams because I never seemed able to have quite made the grade. On reaching school that morning my friend, Margaret, was on the top step at the school gate, her face beaming with smiles. "Well, haven't you heard?" she asked me as I arrived as usual. Nearly all those who had sat the exam had passed, proving that this small church school had reached a very high standard.

CHAPTER V
Between Primary and Grammar Schools

Our primary school days were coming to an end and six glorious weeks of holiday were approaching. Life during wartime was easing in Birmingham. All the days seemed to be fine and sunny for us fortunate children. There were no holidays away but we always found plenty to do to keep us occupied. I had roller skates and would skate up and down the pavement flagstones for ages. When Mother went shopping "round the corner" I would accompany her and once, meeting a neighbour, I was very amused when she remarked how suddenly I had grown so tall. She had not realised I was elevated on my skates.

My bike was my joy as I could ride off anywhere in safety as there was very little traffic. Not so many people owned a car and petrol was still rationed. It was a lovely ride to go down Cherry Orchard Road onto the main road into Birmingham, over the bridge at Great Barr station then along the road past the last few houses on this Northern boundary of Birmingham before riding along the country lane past the Jubilee Colliery which was noisy and black with coal dust. On I would go up to the fields and farm on Hilltop. Here was the view over the countryside to Smethwick and the industrial Black Country in the distance.

I spent hours with a ball. I would go out onto the pavement at the front of the house and practise throwing the ball over the telegraph wires. We did not have underground telephone cables then, all the telephone posts had wires stretched from one to another. This was a long time before mobile phones were invented. The instrument – the telephone – stood on the table in the hall. It was columnar with a mouth piece at the top and the earpiece lodged in a bracket at the side. The dial at the base of the column had letters and numbers. Our number was NOR 1546 indicating we were on the Northern District line long before the invention of mobile phones.

I would not go out when the local boys who lived round about came into the bluebell wood opposite as they would find things to throw at me and tease me. I would never go out when these boys were around.

We children both at school, and my friends who came to play at home would skip with our skipping ropes, turning the rope forwards for as many times as possible before catching our foot on the rope. We would turn the rope backwards and forwards with crossed arms and open arms alternately. With hands together holding the rope we would circle the rope on our right side, then open arms for a skip before turning the rope in a circle on our left side, open arms to skip again. Then we would do "doublers" both forwards and backwards which meant turning the rope twice while jumping over it once only. We would run and skip over the rope turning it as we ran. With more friends we could have one holding each end of the rope, turning it as we skipped saying jingles such as "Salt, pepper, mustard, vinegar" and running in and out of the rope as it was turned. Another skipping game was to have someone snake the rope on the ground by waving it backwards and forwards while we jumped over it trying not to get caught by it. Sometimes we would use the rope for jumping practice. Friends would hold the rope at each end and gradually raise it for us to jump over higher and higher.

There would be days out when Mother would pack a picnic and we would go on the bus to Dudley Zoo. It was a very large zoo outside the Birmingham area and we would spend all day there seeing all the animals in their various cages and enclosures. I liked the polar bears, sea lions and penguins best. If we arrived at the enclosures at an appointed time we could watch the zoo keeper feeding the animals. We would follow him from enclosure to enclosure entranced.

Another day we would go to the Botanical Gardens, a large area inside Birmingham city boundary with trees, paths and green places where we could run and play. Mother would enjoy the flowers and gardens but we were more interested in the cages with smaller animals, monkeys and birds. There were far fewer to see than at the zoo. I did not enjoy it here as much as at Dudley Zoo which was very much larger.

Sometimes we would go into town, Birmingham, on the bus. This was a treat. The fare for Mother was 4d. and for

Elizabeth and me our fares were a Child's 1½d. (a penny-halfpenny) ticket which the conductress snatched from her ticket rack and punched in her ticket machine with a "ting". I held on to that ticket all the way into town in case the inspector got on the bus wanting to check all tickets.

A 1½d. ticket for the journey to town

One shop I liked to go to was Lewis's. It had a pets' corner on the fourth floor. There was a cage with kittens and another with rabbits and others with birds. As we walked through the store we would hear music being played. There were seats where customers could rest and have a cup of tea and here a lady dressed in a long, formal, black gown would be sitting at the grand piano playing such wonderful music. I did want to stop and listen. There was no taped music then, no canned music being relayed all day long.

In the food department here they sold broken biscuits at a reduced price so we had a bag of those. But best of all were the individual trifles they sold in white, waxy cartons, sponge soaked in jelly with synthetic cream on top. I begged Mother to buy us one each at 6d. each, and what joy we had when she agreed. We could not wait to get home to enjoy them. There was never any question of eating whilst walking, or eating in the street!

After a tiring day in the fresh air Mother made sure we went to bed at a sensible time, Elizabeth first as she was younger, me a little later as befitted my age. Mother's maxim was "Early to bed, early to rise" (which I invariably did) "makes a man healthy, wealthy and wise". The first of these was certainly applicable as to the rest, I had my doubts. She would come upstairs to wish us goodnight. I was not always tired and ready for sleep so, after she had put out our light, I would snuggle down in my bed with my torch in order to read my book under the bed clothes. There was no knowing when she would decide to come and check on us. On hearing footsteps climbing the stairs I would quickly resurface so innocently before diving down again once she had gone.

Unable to get off to sleep I would play a game thinking of all the neighbours in the road. Oh! We knew everyone. I would say the house numbers, 74 backwards up the road to 56. We had just ten semi-detached houses in the road so it was strange to have numbers from 74 to 56. But Worlds End Road was L-shaped and we were in the "foot" part; the "leg" part with the lower numbers having turned the corner at the top of the road and travelled up to the main road. The last "semis" were the Maddens, whose two boys, Michael and Geoffrey, had been evacuated with me at the beginning of the war, then ourselves, the Yardleys. Then came the Pritchards. (One Sunday morning Father was bemused when, answering a knock on the front door, he was confronted by a very small four-year-old neighbour called Malcolm Pritchard who asked, "Can Shederbeff play when Shederbeff's had Shederbeff's breakfast?" – Shederbeff being his effort at the tongue twister "Elizabeth".) Miss Parkin lived next door to the Pritchards with her father. The Miss Moyles, two sisters, both head mistresses of whom I was rather in awe, and Mrs. Bull came next. The following two semis were occupied by Mrs. Sargent (a widow) and the Whitehouses, where Margaret, who played with Elizabeth, lived, and last came Mrs. Evans and Mrs. Galloway, the lady who thought I had grown tall so quickly since she had not noticed I was on my roller skates.

In my game I would recite these neighbours and their numbers backwards, forwards and alternately and any other way which would eventually send me off to sleep.

There had been tragedies in the road, as happens everywhere. In the very early days of us all moving into these new houses, next door to us at Number 70, Mr. Nuttage had committed suicide by hanging himself from the banister. I knew of this later as being only very young at the time it did not mean anything to me. Now, it is often said that some houses are jinxed and it would seem so with number 70. It was after my evacuation and our return to our house that we discovered our neighbours in number 70 were the Goldens. They had a little boy, Hughie. Why Hughie had been allowed to ride his tricycle on the landing upstairs I will never know but the worst happened. Hughie came downstairs fatally from top to bottom. He was just three.

Another trauma happened on the other side of us at number 74. The first we knew of it was when the fire engines arrived. In all the commotion we saw smouldering bedding, sheets, pillow, mattress, being thrown out of the front bedroom window onto the front lawn below. It seems Mr. Madden was in the habit of smoking cigarettes in bed and it must have been a spark or hot ash which ignited and set fire to his bed. He survived.

CHAPTER VI
Introducing the Grammar School

In 1944 the war was coming to an end although London was still suffering raids. We in Birmingham had a much easier time. Nevertheless, rationing was still in force.

It was now time to embark on my secondary education. Several girls from my primary school, including my best friend Margaret, were joining me at King Edwards's Grammar School for Girls, Handsworth. During the holidays Mother had taken me into town to kit me out in my new school uniform. We all had to wear navy blue, A-line gymslips, no pleats, with white, square-necked blouses underneath, and the inevitable navy blue knickers. It was Autumn 1944. I was eleven years old. When I started we all wore brown, lisle stockings with suspenders to keep them up. Oh dear! What a predicament and how unfortunate I was when my suspender broke and my stocking was starting to fall down. The immediate solution was to walk with my hand in my pocket trying to grab the stocking top to keep my stocking up. What a lopsided walk I invented!

Lopsided Walk – Broken Suspender

We had sensible, brown, lace-up shoes which always had to be clean and polished each day. Trainers were unheard of then. Hats were compulsory, navy blue, brimmed felt hats with grossgrain ribbon hatband of blue and green, correctly worn with blue above and green below. At the age of eleven my young senses were appalled at putting the colours green and blue together, but, as I matured, my artistic vision improved and I realised how nature intervened: the sky was blue, the grass green, so what could be more natural. The choice of colour for our hatband was not so bad after all, in retrospect! A navy mackintosh would complete the outfit. This was our winter wear. When summer came we had to change into cotton dresses with short sleeves. A school rule was no sleeveless dresses. We could wear white ankle socks and brown sandals and, for our head gear, a panama hat with the hatband. A school blazer with the school badge embroidered on the pocket was a must. We were always very smart.

There was one rule regarding hair. If it reached our shoulders it must be tied back. This was no problem for me. I had plaits. Every girl had to have a turkey red cotton drawstring bag with her name embroidered on it in white chain stitch. Mother made mine. In this would be carried a pair of white plimsolls for sport and a pair of brown bar shoes with a button fastening which each girl had to change into from her outdoor shoes every morning. Indoor shoes were a must and the bag had to be hung on each girl's allotted peg in the cloakroom.

The first morning was very scary. All the new girls were following each other along Rose Hill Road and were being marshalled through the school gates, round the path and into the large room on the ground floor, the playroom. It was in here that everyone congregated on wet playtimes when the weather prevented us from going outside into the playground, past the tennis courts and beneath the sweet chestnut trees. It was in the following few years in the autumn that I would aim to be first out at break to find the lovely plump sweet chestnuts which had fallen to the ground. No need to save them to roast in hot ashes. I would peel and crunch them there and then.

This first morning we sat on the playroom floor in rows waiting to be told which form we would be in. The clever girls who passed well in the entrance exam went into form III A. They were to be taught Latin. The next cleverest went into III Alpha and they were also taught Latin. My friend Margaret from Church Hill Road went into this form. I was put into form III b which was destined to be taught German, and the last form, III Beta, was where girls did home crafts. Of course the timetable included much else besides.

All the girls in the school were grouped into Houses and many competitions were fought out amongst the Houses to determine which would win first place and the cup each year. The Houses were named after the Royal Houses: Windsor, Stuart, Normandy, Hanover, Plantagenet, Tudor, York and Lancaster. I was put into Hanover.

We were then taken up the stairs, along the lower corridor to our form room. It was a surprise to find here that we had our own single desk, with attached tip-up seat. All were arranged in rows facing the large, wall-mounted blackboard. No easels with blackboards here. Everything was so different.

The school had a large, beautifully decorated central hall with a platform at the top end where the headmistress took assembly each morning. This hall was two storeys high. There was the lower, tiled corridor and the upper tiled corridor with windows all along between these corridors and the hall. On Speech Days, when visitors and parents of prize winners arrived to swell the numbers, these windows upstairs were removed and benches placed alongside so that girls in the lower forms could sit up there, in silence, and watch proceedings down below, joining in the singing at the appropriate time.

There were special rooms for science, art, music and cookery as well as the dining room and kitchens. Alongside the playroom on the ground floor were the gymnasium and cloakrooms. It was a magnificent school. It was here that I was to spend seven happy years.

CHAPTER VII
Lessons

School days were governed by bells: bells to go down to the hall for assembly and bells for the end of each lesson. Some lessons were taken in our own form room, for others, such as science, music or art, we had to move, en bloc, to another room. Bells rang for morning playtime, or break as we now called it, when there was an added delight, a bun. Each morning the porter would stand in the entrance corridor with a large baker's tray before him on which were buns priced at 1d. (one penny) plain ones or some with jam in the centre. I would always try to be one of the first down there to claim a jam bun.

As juniors we had two lessons before our break and three afterwards to ease the congestion. The seniors had three lessons before their break which came half-an-hour after ours, and two lessons after. The school day began at 9.00 a.m. We all had to be there by 8.55 a.m. and the morning session ended at 1.00 p.m. Afternoon lessons, just two as a general rule, began at 2.20 p.m. and we finished at 3.50 p.m. Thursday was our half day, always looked forward to. We also had an afternoon of sport each week. The sports field was a bus ride away as there was no ground available for pitches at the school itself. There were two tennis courts here at school and here they also played netball, whereas hockey in winter and rounders in summer needed more space. The sports field was next door to Bradford's Bakery and when the wind blew in our direction over the windy heights the smell of baking bread was wonderful. We had such exhilarating afternoons.

As the years progressed I found myself in the hockey second team. How I longed to be awarded a second team girdle, a green braid to wear around the waist, to tie in a knot and have the tails hanging down the back of my gymslip, but awards were made and my name did not appear. I always played in the same position as the first team captain, centre half, and she never missed a practice or a match so I could not get any first team experience, therefore I suppose I was not good enough. Nevertheless my name was called out. I had been awarded a posture stripe! So Mother's persistence of "hold your head up, back straight" did pay dividends after all. I was awarded an insignificant strip of yellow braid to sew onto a black braid to wear round my waist. I never wore it!

I enjoyed the lessons. In our second year, when we were now in form Lower IVB, we had needlework with Miss Martin, during which we made a dress for ourselves. The material was supplied by school with a minimal choice of colours as there were still shortages. The material was cotton. Polycotton or polyester had not yet arrived. I chose a green and white with flowers over a check design. All through those lessons Miss Martin read a book to us. We were so quiet and industrious. We must have done our sewing very well, all by hand as there were no sewing machines supplied. When our dresses were finished we had to wear them and present ourselves to the headmistress. As I was about to go down to her room, Joan stopped me and re-tied my belt at the back, saying the bow was not quite right. Now Joan, one of my class mates, had a magic touch because when it came to the prize giving on speech day I was one of the prize winners, sitting down in the hall with visitors and parents. Mother was in the audience, to see me go up onto the platform to receive my prize for needlework. That was my one and only prize. I received a book by Noel Streatfield called "Ballet Shoes", which Mother had suggested as I had had ballet lessons now for several years.

Needlework Prize

There were more light-hearted lessons too. At least I thought so. The art class produced some unusual results, especially when Miss Ward gave us the idea of painting pictures all over furniture. It was not quite graffiti but the forerunner! What on earth would my parents think if I painted pictures on our furniture at home? Miss Ward was before her time as the expression goes, as soon to follow was white wood furniture which needed decoration. After the dullness and gloom of war these ideas brought colour back into our lives.

My light-heartedness sometimes caused me trouble for on one day I was in a very frivolous mood. It was the day for the music lesson and we all trooped off to the music room where bench seats were arranged in tiers in the auditorium. It was the lecture theatre. The piano was down on the floor at the front. Here sat Miss Pritchard who had decided she would play a phrase on the piano and each one of us individually would sing an appropriate ending. She was testing our music ability.

Now here I will digress a little to mention my younger sister Elizabeth. Elizabeth was musical and was always singing. Did this talent spring from when Mother would always sing her to sleep every night from the time when she was so ill? She must have developed it as Mother sang to her when she was small. Whilst in the country during our evacuation, visiting the doctor, she sang in the waiting room to the delight of the other patients. She was only four years old and sang one of Mother's lullabies:-

"I had a little nut tree, nothing would it bear
But a silver nutmeg and a golden pear.
The Queen of Spain's daughter came to visit me
And all was because of my little nut tree."

On hearing her singing the doctor called her in and asked her to sing it again for him, whereupon be brought out a packet of sweets, rationed sweets, for her to choose one. At a very early age she was playing tunes on her recorder. But she not only played on a proper instrument. We found her playing "God Save the King" on the egg slicer as she plucked the wires! When a little older she was asked by Mother to put some meat away in the pantry. Later, after hunting high and low along the pantry shelves, unable to find it, she asked Elizabeth where she had put it. Elizabeth could not tell her as she did not know. It was later found on top of the piano where she had dropped it when she had stopped to play something she had just thought of.

As I have said, my sister Elizabeth was musical. I was not! She was always singing, often asking me to sing something with her while she harmonised! So, when Miss Pritchard called me out for my turn to sing the end of the phrase she played on the piano, I did not do like everyone else but sang notes which would harmonise, as I thought. Miss Pritchard looked at me, shaking her head: "Oh, no, no!" It was not a good idea at all. Well, further into the lesson we had to write a musical phrase in our music notebook. As I have said, music was not my forte. I made mistakes and crossed them out, making rather a mess of my attempt. All the books were collected for marking. Oh dear!

And when mine came back the comment written on the bottom was: "Re-write the whole of this page." This I did, lock, stock and barrel: in its entirety! A complete copy, including the comment, a perfect copy, mistakes and all! Well, it was what was asked for! My Word! Was my exuberance trimmed down! No doubt about it. When Mother received my end of term report she came across:-

"Conduct: Ann can behave very well. She must learn to distinguish between fun and naughtiness."

I did not like history and my marks were often low, just passes. Comments on my reports were "Ann could do better" and "Ann is content with a poor standard of work." The history mistress was not my favourite mistress and I was horrified one year to find she was to be our form mistress. For one term of that year I was voted form captain and it so happened during that term that she fell ill and was off school. It was voted that we would collect money for a bouquet of flowers for her and, as form captain, it fell to me to take them to her house. It was not a chore I enjoyed or looked forward to but one always has to do something one does not want to do! At the end of this term her report on my conduct was "Very good. Ann has discharged her duties as form captain reliably and well." I did not dislike her quite so much afterwards.

In contrast to this mistress, I loved the geography teacher, mainly because she awarded me a star for neatness in my geography notebook. It was the only star I ever won. The stars were collected at the end of each term and added up at the end of the year. A cup was awarded to the House with the most points.

During the second year we had a double period of cooking each week in the domestic science room. Prior to this, in the needlework class, we had all made aprons with bibs in preparation for this activity. All were hand sewn, green and white check cotton with waistband and neck strap. Across the front of the bib we all had to have our name prominently embroidered in white chain stitch. As to the cookery, it is strange how one only remembers the failures! It was in the Christmas term and we made pastry for a plate mince pie. This class was during the last two periods of the afternoon. The class was large and the uncooked pies went into the ovens in relays. I was one of the last to have mine put in the oven. It was getting late. The bell would shortly be going for the end of the afternoon school when there was a mad rush to get out and on to the buses before the long queues were formed. My pie was not cooked so the oven was turned up to hurry it along. The result was a burnt mince pie and the grade for my effort was all but fail. It was the teacher who had turned up the oven.

Throughout the school year there were many competitions, the results of which provided points awarded towards the House cups. The House captains would visit all the forms chivvying the pupils to enter the various competitions. I nearly always entered the wild flower competition. My previous years spent in the country gave me an interest in all nature. The science mistress arranged jam jars along one of the benches in the science laboratory, each one containing a wild flower which we had to identify, writing it down on a prepared form with our name, form and House. There were about twenty species but none with which I was familiar. There were never any flowers I was used to seeing in the country, no purple orchids, ox-eyed daisies, marsh marigolds which we called king cups, or lords and ladies (our far more attractive name for arums). I was flummoxed by the enormous genus of the cabbage family such as the common yellow hedgerow flowers known as wild cabbage, hedge mustard, wall rocket and charlock, which were put out for us to identify. I never learned the names of all the different varieties. However, I did my best and, with a few points, helped towards the coveted cup.

The music competition came along, when each House would provide a choir to sing two songs before an adjudicator. All girls were chivvied as usual. We practised but we did not have a conductor and a conductor was necessary. No-one would volunteer. I had, by this time, just gone into the VIth form and some demon spirit inside me was driving me to offer, telling me someone must step forward and do it. With all my limited music ability I said I would have a go! I had been to concerts and was fascinated by the conductor's antics waving his arms about.

All I needed to do was the same with a baton in my hand. I had had dancing lessons for several years now and been in shows. Always PRESENTATION was stressed. "You must look as though you are enjoying yourselves and SMILE." So the choir was encouraged to look as though it was enjoying itself singing the songs, to open their mouths and smile. Before them I did my best to produce this pleasurable effect. I waved my arms, smiled at them for encouragement and pointed my baton, except I did not have a baton. The only thing I could think to use was one of my knitting needles. I was a great knitter! Here was I, conducting with my knitting needle, thankfully with no knitting on it! All the choirs gathered during the afternoon to hear the adjudicator's verdict. The results were announced. First, second, third, fourth, fifth, sixth, and Hanover seventh. Well, at least we were not last and I had stepped in in my fashion when no-one else would volunteer.

The staff at King Edward VI Grammar School, Handsworth, assembled on the front steps. Among them are: Miss Bardhill, Miss Anderson, Miss Warren, Mrs. Udall, Mrs. Greenwood, Miss Hyde, Miss Evans, Miss Miller, Miss Bamforth, Miss Isaacs, Miss Jeffries, Miss Pritchard, Mrs. Jameson, Miss Innis, Miss Burchill, Miss Naish, Miss Tolley, Miss Stewart.

CHAPTER VIII
Home Life

School life was very full and life at home was just as full and busy. We economised wherever it was possible. One government incentive was "Dig up your front lawn and grow your own vegetables," so our front lawn was dug up and given over to cabbages. There were shortages everywhere. Meat was rationed and anything to help out was tried. Father's cousin, whom we called Uncle Howard, was considering building a pen at the end of his garden and installing a pig which would not only provide meat but would eat up all the household leftovers. When grown and fattened it could be slaughtered: half of it Uncle could keep for his own use and half must be handed over to the authorities. This did not quite materialise as the neighbours complained, imagining the awesome smell of pig manure invading their houses.

Father decided he would try his hand at poultry keeping. Alongside the swing he built a henhouse with enclosed hen run, and installed six laying hens. For months now eggs had been scarce and, as everyone else had done, Mother had used dried egg in her cooking. Now we should be able to have an occasional real egg. The hens had to be shut in the hen house every evening and let out into the run every morning. They had to have a dish of grit to help in the making of the egg shells and a receptacle for water for drinking. They had several handfuls of corn thrown into the pen each day and cabbage stalks with some leaves (of which we had plenty on the front "lawn") hung up just out of their reach so that they had exercise in jumping to reach them! Any left-over greens from the house were also thrown in for them. Then came their evening meal, and here Father excelled himself! All scraps of food were saved: nothing was ever wasted or thrown away if a use could be found for it. Vegetable peelings were treasured and put into a pressure cooker to cook them FOR THE HENS. There was no pressure cooker for our use. When the set time was reached and the peelings cooked, the shrill whistle from the pot blew. Father would removed the pressure cooker from the gas ring on the cooker and gradually undo the screw top to release the hot steam which hissed as it streamed out. The contents were then mashed together with handfuls of bran and this warm concoction was fed to the greedy hens who could not wait for it. They would run up and down the pen, necks stretching, squawking away, anxious to get at this foul-smelling food. (I was Father's helper, as was Mother. As he was not always at home to attend to the fowls we had to do this job for him.)

Hungry Hens

I loved going to the nest boxes each day to see if there was an egg waiting there. We generally knew when an egg had been laid as the hen was so proud of her achievement she could not refrain from cackling away, announcing it to anyone in the vicinity. At certain times of the year the hens stopped laying. The hens began to moult and looked poor straggly birds. It was then that a dusting with Derris powder helped. The hens had to be caught and the powder shaken into their feathers and fingered in amongst them to help relieve the irritation and kill off the fleas.

Father came home with a cockerel, for with an amorous cock in with the hens there was every chance that the eggs laid would be fertilised. When a hen became broody she would be encouraged to sit on a clutch of eggs in the nest box and, hey presto, before long we would have little fluffy yellow chickens to boost the numbers. It was not long before Father decided that the cock would make a fine meal. It was still wartime and other meat was scarce. How I would miss his crowing.

Whilst living in the country before returning home to Birmingham I had watched Mother skinning a rabbit. Rabbits had sometimes been given to us by the farmer. After removing the entrails Mother would have to draw each limb from its furry covering, dismember it and chop off its head before making it ready for a sustaining rabbit stew. Now she had to be prepared

48

to deal with the cockerel after Father had slit its throat and hung it up on a nail outside to bleed. Mother sat outside with a cover on the ground before her, her apron tied around her and a scarf tied over her hair in readiness to begin plucking all the feathers off the bird. The feathers flew everywhere and by the time she was finished, hot and tired, she herself was smothered in feathers, clinging to her eyebrows and tickling her nose. It was proposed that the feathers would make a good soft filling for a pillow or cushion but they would first have to be sterilised. I think this was one economy we did not make. The meal of cooked cock had to suffice.

Feathers everywhere

There came a day when Mother heard that the greengrocer round the corner had some bananas. Bananas had not been seen since the beginning of the war. He would be selling them at a certain time. A quick run round to the shop showed her that word had spread very quickly and a queue had formed. Each customer was allotted them according to the number of ration books she held.

Another day I returned home from school and Mother handed me a basin. Would I run round to the shops as she had heard there was some icecream to be had. I came home with several scoops full, running fast to arrive home before the icecream melted.

And so war time progressed towards its end.

CHAPTER IX
With Father

Father was no longer required to work for the Ministry of Aviation, ferrying aero parts from the manufacturer to the assembly point, so he returned to his normal occupation of furniture remover. He and his brother, my Uncle Norman, had the family removal business, each driving one of three vans, a large one, a medium one and one slightly smaller.

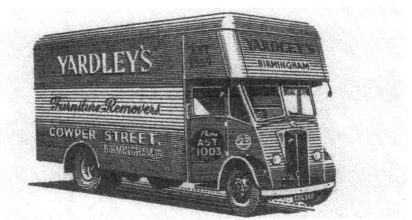

Father's Van

We rarely saw Father during the week. He was always in bed when we left for school and we were always in bed when he returned home. He could not begin the removals early as his customers would not be ready and packed up. The removal lasted until the last piece of furniture was off the van. Then the van had to be tidied up and swept out with all the webbing ties firmly in place ready for the next day. He then returned to base, which was Grandfather's home, and then the day's booking had to be done and the morrow's jobs arranged. If a journey was necessary the route had to be planned and maps studied. He was always late home, often after eleven o'clock at night. Saturday was also a working day, aiming to end at one o'clock, which rarely happened.

At this time many families owned a piano and Father found much of his time was taken up doing removals for a piano shop in Birmingham. He would often be called upon to move concert pianos into the concert hall, and so the firm displayed "Piano Removal Specialists" after "Furniture Removers." Father could "play by ear" and whenever he loaded a piano onto the van he would try it out to make sure it was alright by standing before it playing tunes on it before tying it in safely. Many are the times he acquired an audience in the road at the back of the van drawn to listen to this musical interlude.

The comedy pair "Laurel and Hardy" made an amusing film in which they struggled unsuccessfully to move a piano upstairs but it kept eluding their grasp and slipping down the stairs. Often Father's piano removals called for the removal of a piano to an upstairs room but not in the fashion of Laurel and Hardy! Father had block and tackle and ladders. The operation often required the removal of an upstairs window so that the roped piano could be drawn up the ladders to enter through the upstairs window space. It was a heavy day's work. But when moving a piano just from one room to another, or just re-positioning it in the same room, a small leather- covered, four-wheeled trolley was used. I know! An occasional weekend job would come up and Father would ask me to give him a hand. Placing the trolley alongside the side of the piano (an upright piano that is, as a grand piano removal was different altogether) Father would then tip up the piano onto the trolley which rocked to accept it. I was just required to steady it. It was then wheeled to its new position in the room or into another room where it would be placed and righted. For this assistance I earned 2/6d (two shillings and sixpence, or half-a-crown) 25p in today's money.

Coins Before Decimalisation
Top Row: half crown 2/6, florin 2/-, sixpence 6d.
2nd Row: shilling 1/-, shilling 1/-, 3 penny piece 3d.
3rd Row: one penny 1d., half penny ½d., farthing ¼d.

During the school holidays, when Father had to make a journey of some distance, I would ask if I could go with him. It was wonderful for me, sitting high up in the cab from where I had marvellous views of all the scenery. One memorable journey was over the desolate, barren Yorkshire moors. The weather was dull and windy. It was such an atmospheric journey with the wind whistling through the windscreen. I loved to knit and this day I took my knitting with me for now I could knit without looking at it as long as there was no pattern. I remember the wool was blue and the pattern was for a dress for my twelve-inch doll. The hem of the dress had a block pattern of garter stitch and stocking stitch. I completed all the knitting, back and front and short puff sleeves, during that day in the van.

To make up for not seeing us during the week, and now that petrol rationing was easing, Father would take us out for a drive in the car on Sunday afternoons. Sunday mornings would find him out in the garden, digging, which he loved to do after a hard week's work. Mother was often cross with him for not changing his clothes when he came in at Sunday lunch time when we all sat in the dining room for our Sunday lunch, but afterwards he was soon ready to take us out.

One Sunday we set off for Malvern where we would walk on the Malvern Hills. I was like a mountain goat scrambling everywhere, and where I went Elizabeth was sure to follow. We were quite a long way up a path when little Elizabeth slipped and down, down, down she rolled, unable to stop herself. Mother and Father were aghast, white faced, standing at the bottom. They picked her up and laid her on the back seat of the car. I clambered in beside. We returned home. Elizabeth recovered. She appeared to be none the worse for her experience, though bruised. There was no National Health then so visits to the doctor were not made unless absolutely necessary.

On other Sunday afternoon drives we would always look out for a shop which was selling icecream, begging Father to stop and buy one, but more often than not he found it impossible to park, such were the queues for this long awaited treat.

Sunday nights were times we really looked forward to. After tea Father would come and sit with us in the lounge by the fire and produce several packs of cards. We would choose which game we wanted to play that night; Menu, Speed, Happy Families. Mother would sit knitting and listening. She disliked card games and recalled the time in the country when she made up the numbers really against her will, winning the booby prize, which turned out to be a hundredweight of Swedes.

CHAPTER X
My Friend Freda

From the time when I first returned home from evacuation in the country I renewed my friendship with a pre-war playmate named Freda. Freda's parents had not wanted her to be evacuated so she stayed at home and went to a different primary school. Her mother and my mother had been friends before the war started. Together they had begun the Mother's Union meetings for our estate.

Freda was the first one to speak to me on our return as she saw me over the front fence swinging on our "gallows". She called, "You're back then!" She was one of the children who had come to my early birthday parties, the high point of which was when we had all sat cross-legged, after our party tea, on the floor of the back room where Father had set up a screen and projector which he had hired. And there we had all clapped and laughed at the antics of Mickey Mouse and Donald Duck. There was no such thing as television to watch.

Freda was about a year older than me. After my first year at the grammar school we would cycle there together most days. First-year pupils were not allowed to go on their bikes owing to the shortage of space in the cycle shed. During the first year we always travelled on the bus. There was a short walk after we left the bus, along a tram route and, if we were late, a short tram ride rattling up the road to school was a boon. As we left the tram we would come to the sweet shop – tuck shop, we called it. But we were never allowed to venture inside. School rules said it was out of bounds. No-one ever ate in the street in those days. There was therefore no litter, no sweet papers dropped. Drinks cans were not heard of. You would never drink in the street. Large glass bottles of lemonade could be bought for home use. For every glass bottle returned to the shop we would earn 1d. (one penny) so there were no bottles left lying about. Plastic had not been invented. The pennies earned boosted our pocket money.

From the second year at the grammar school I rode my bike to school. I now had a larger one as I had outgrown my first one and this one had three speeds. I also had a dynamo fitted to the back wheel and when the lamps were switched on front and back, as darkness descended, the speed at which I pedalled and the wheels turned regulated the brightness of the light. The faster I went the brighter the light! I had a saddle bag at the back which contained a repair kit in case I had a puncture, and a basket on the front strapped to the handlebars. This was far more useful than the saddlebag which had to be strapped shut. The basket in front could be fully laden and I could ride using one hand on the handlebars, the other holding everything likely to fall off.

Full Bike Basket

Freda lived in Cherry Orchard Road at the bottom of the hill and many are the times I have waited on the corner outside our house to see her appearing in the distance. Invariably she was late and after reaching me out of breath, we would pedal furiously to get to school on time. This was mostly at dinner time for we always returned home to dinner at mid-day. It was wonderful cycling home down a hill, the wind blowing in my face, making the journey as fast as possible. When entering our road I was certain I could smell the dinner Mother had ready and was just waiting until I arrived before putting it on the table.

While riding to school Freda and I would discuss what lessons we had had and what was on that day's agenda. Freda was doing cookery – cheese dreams. They sounded wonderful

56

so I asked Mother if Freda could come to our house and show me how to make them. Mother agreed to give us the run of the kitchen. And what were cheese dreams? Nothing more than cheese sandwiches fried in the frying pan in a little lard. They tasted delicious, juice oozing out of the bread. We had done them ourselves and Mother wondered whether or not we would make ourselves sick.

Through Freda I learnt to make pastry, very light and more-ish. We made it in our kitchen. Whereas when I had been allowed to make it I rolled the rolling pin backwards and forwards several times to flatten the pastry, Freda said, "Miss McClure said you must roll the pastry once one way only, then lift the rolling pin before rolling again, turning the pastry round as you go and making sure it does not stick to the board, thus rolling it thinner as you progress." And what Miss McClure said, we did! Our pastry was perfect.

I wanted to make another dress after my success in the Lower IVth form. Mother bought me the material, a green and white striped cotton. I chose a pattern but I really wanted a "sweetheart" neckline. This was neither straight nor round but had a curvey V shape.

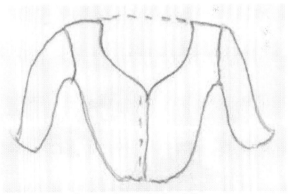

Sweetheart Neckline

I told Freda as we cycled along and she said she knew how to alter it to what I wanted. We set ourselves up in the back room on the dining table and she produced some brown paper. This paper was placed under the pattern piece which I wanted altered and she drew round the pattern. After removing the pattern she

57

drew the shape I wanted on the brown paper, exactly as I said I wanted it, cut it out and, hey presto! I had my new pattern. Freda was a genius!

Ann and Freda Clearing Snow

It was during the winter evenings that I started our Busy Bee Club. Knitting was popular and I asked Freda and two friends, both called Margaret, if they would like to come to our house every week and we would knit. Mother joined us as did our next door neighbour, Mrs. Madden, who was a great knitter, always knitting Fair Isle. Mrs. Sargent, the widow from number 62 up the road, also came as she was always interested in what we did. We would have refreshments, natter and knit and I made badges for us all to wear when we came once a week to our Busy Bee Club. To this day my friends still talk of the lovely evenings we had.

Elizabeth, and Ann wearing a Fair Isle Jumper made by Mrs. Madden

CHAPTER XI
Girl Guides

Freda, the two Margarets and I joined the Girl Guides. We met every Thursday evening in the church hall and Freda and I would cycle there leaving our bikes in the entrance hall. Our uniform consisted of a blue, collared, long-sleeved, straight tunic with two breast pockets which bulged with notebook, pen, handkerchief and anything else we wanted to carry.

Girl Guide Uniform

Around our waist we wore a brown leather belt with a buckle carrying the Girl Guide badge. At the side swung our penknife and anything else we needed as good Girl Guides. Our tie was triangular in two pieces sewn together, one green and one orange, and it had to be folded precisely so that the orange was down the front, the green made the knot under the chin and the two ends tied at the back under the collar in a reef knot, ends tucked in so as not to be visible. The tie had to be tied and worn so that there were three fingers' width between the bottom of the tie and the top of the belt. Our hats were dark blue felt with a brim, and our shoes were brown. Oh, we were very smart. Each Thursday before the meeting I would be found in the kitchen with the ironing board in front of me ironing my tunic so that it was creaseless. When worn it had to be smooth at the back and front, all slack being folded into a pleat at the side of the waist. The hat brim must be stiff. This was achieved by ironing the brim beneath brown paper. The brown shoes were polished till they shone, even under the instep where the soles met the heels. The soles of our shoes would always be on view whenever we knelt down.

Guides and Brownies in Uniform

Our Captain was a stickler for neatness. She was the District Commissioner and wore her uniform with its long jacket and her cockaded hat with pride.

Commissioners in their Uniforms but not our Captain

We were smart. Hair had always to be tied back if it was long enough to touch our collar. This was no problem for me. I had plaits! So much for appearance.

We were put into groups – patrols - everyone being given a round floral embroidered badge to sew onto her tunic. I was in the Scarlet Pimpernel patrol and whenever I see one of these tiny plants growing in the garden I think of the days when I joined the Girl Guides. Each patrol had a leader with two white stripes on her pocket and a seconder with one white stripe on her pocket. Each patrol had a "corner" to set up with appropriate literature and nature specimens suitable for the patrol's interest. The corner displays were inspected by the captain and her Lieutenant and were awarded first, second, third and fourth places. We played games, learnt to tie knots, did simple first aid such as bandaging and the use of slings, and we sang songs. Midway through the evening our patrols were lined up for inspection and the patrol leader collected our subscription for the day, 1d. (one penny). There were generally about seven girls in each patrol. I progressed through the ranks, becoming a seconder for my patrol then a leader to take on another patrol. This was Fuchsia patrol.

We had outings and I remember one winter's outing into the country led by "Lefty" whose fiancé accompanied us. What a brave man Bernard was! How we enjoyed his company. The outing stands out for me because we walked over brown frosted fields in all the hard ruts in glorious winter sunshine.

Once we were taken for a week-end stay in a small hotel on the riverside at Bewdley. I had friends other than Freda in the troop, the two Margarets. All my friends seemed to be called Margaret at that time. One became my life-long friend in the primary school, the other was my life-long friend linked from birth since our mothers were next-door neighbours and remained close friends. Even during evacuation this Margaret and her mother lived in Nene Sollars which is in the same church diocese as Knighton-on-Teme where we were. At the time of the Bewdley trip, Elizabeth, my sister, had just joined the Guides and came with us on the week-end away. When it came to our bed time I was in a double bed with Margaret but Elizabeth was in another room and was not at all happy at being away from her big sister. She was so very tearful and wanted to be with me so we ended up that night sleeping three in the bed, Margaret, Elizabeth in the middle and me.

We went to camp, under canvas. We learnt to dig latrines, to build camp fires and cook in a billy can. I was so enthusiastic with all aspects of Guiding that I had to practice at home. Father was persuaded to buy us a small tent which we erected on the lawn at the back of the house and where Elizabeth and I slept outside overnight, much to Mother's consternation. I had learnt to build a proper camp fire so that had to be practised down at the bottom of the garden.

Elizabeth in front, Ann behind, Margaret left, making a fire in the garden

Fortunately I did not want to dig a trench. We did have an outside toilet! Margaret came to practise with me and our activity aroused the curiosity of Michael next door so he came round to have a closer inspection.

Michael came to inspect

I had learnt to tie all the knots; reef knot, fisherman's knot, bowline, clove hitch and so on. They were distributed all over the house.

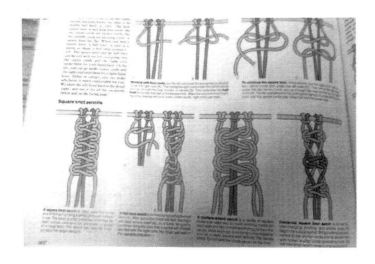

It was not surprising, therefore, a little later on in my Guiding experience when we had to make lanyards, that the dining room furniture was brought into use. Lanyards were made of white cord, slipped over our head, the ends joined in front with a turk's head knot. The braid extended at the end, to which would be attached a whistle which was then hooked onto the belt at the side. The lanyard was made by twisting the white cord in macramé fashion using the different macramé patterns and whilst in construction the dining room chairs had to be commandeered so that I could loop the cord around them.

Making macramé knots for a lanyard
The dining room had to be carefully negotiated, especially when the doctor came to visit Elizabeth who was with me while I

twisted. Mother apologised to the doctor for the mess! He was obviously one of my sort for he said he much preferred to see a house full of activity rather than a sterile one where everything looked perfectly in place. It gave me leeway for many activities in the days ahead!

All my activities enabled me to work towards doing the tests for the many badges which could be won. Among those I earned were my health, cooking, laundry, hostess, first aid, knitting, needlewoman, toy making, artist, dancer and poultry keeping.

My Guide Badges
From the top in a clockwise direction:-
Good Housekeeping
First Aid
Artist
Knitting
Needlewoman
Dancer

Toy Maker
Poultry Keeping
Laundry
Cooking
Hostess
Health

I was promoted to Company Leader at about 15 years of age and now wore three white stripes on my pocket.

On certain Sundays throughout the year we had church parade and I was frequently chosen to carry the flag, being a strong, sturdy sort of Guide, always looking very smart.

The Flag Carrier

Freda told me her mother could not understand why I was always chosen to carry the flag, I always wagged my bottom too much! Since when I have developed a walk in which my bottom does not wag and I always make sure it is covered by a long top! We assembled in the road. I had an escort on either side. We processed up the road, through the church yard, into the church, up the aisle and nave right up to the altar where I knelt down whilst the curate relieved me of the flag and stood it against the wall. This was the moment for which the polished soles of our shoes, the instep between the heels and soles, had been prepared, since, when we knelt down, everyone could see the bottom of our shoes.

The evening arrived when the local Boy Scout troop had been invited to join us. They warily entered the room where we awaited them, eyeing them up and down to see what they were like. Games had been planned and prepared. Individually we engineered ourselves towards the smartest looking ones and put on our best performances to attract their attention. Having decided on our preference, when it came to singing the Guide and Scout songs we endeavoured to sit beside or in front of our chosen one. Bobby appealed to me and appeared in my thoughts for quite a while afterwards until other attractions came on the scene.

CHAPTER XII
Dancing Days

Throughout all this time, between 1943 and 1948, I had been attending a dancing school for lessons in ballet, tap and musical comedy. Whilst in the country, between 1940 and 1943, Mother had sent Elizabeth and me to the dancing class in Tenbury Wells with Miss Ferris. It was behind the small market hall at the back of town. Here I was entered, in December 1942, for my first ballet exam, Grade II, but unfortunately we had to leave and return to Birmingham.

Mother now enrolled me in one of the best dancing schools in Birmingham, the Studio School of Dance. The Principal was Madame Helena Lehmiski. She saw me dance the routine for my approaching Grade II exam and shook her head in dismay. It would not do at all. I had to learn another dance in the remaining fortnight. I passed. I was nine years old. Then followed the ballet exams for Grades III and IV during the next twelve months, for both of which I gained honours.

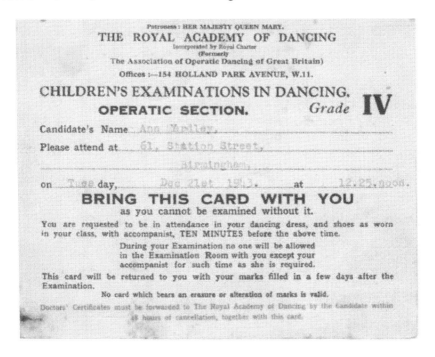

Patroness : HER MAJESTY QUEEN MARY.

THE ROYAL ACADEMY OF DANCING
Incorporated by Royal Charter
(Formerly
The Association of Operatic Dancing of Great Britain)
Offices :—154 HOLLAND PARK AVENUE, W.11.

CHILDREN'S EXAMINATIONS IN DANCING.
OPERATIC SECTION. *Grade* **IV**

Candidate's Name   Ann Miller,

Please attend at   61, Station Street,
Birmingham,

on   Tuesday,   Dec 21st 1943,   at   12.25.noon.

BRING THIS CARD WITH YOU
as you cannot be examined without it.

You are requested to be in attendance in your dancing dress, and shoes as worn in your class, with accompanist, TEN MINUTES before the above time.

During your Examination no one will be allowed in the Examination Room with you except your accompanist for such time as she is required.

This card will be returned to you with your marks filled in a few days after the Examination.

No card which bears an erasure or alteration of marks is valid.

Doctors' Certificates must be forwarded to The Royal Academy of Dancing by the Candidate within 48 hours of cancellation, together with this card.

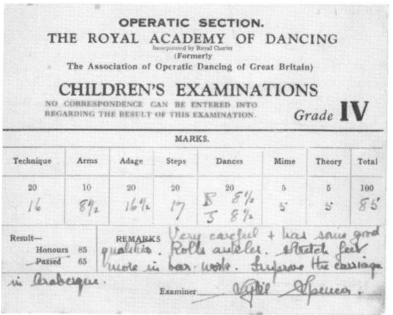

OPERATIC SECTION.

THE ROYAL ACADEMY OF DANCING

(Formerly
The Association of Operatic Dancing of Great Britain)

CHILDREN'S EXAMINATIONS

NO CORRESPONDENCE CAN BE ENTERED INTO
REGARDING THE RESULT OF THIS EXAMINATION.

Grade **IV**

MARKS.

Technique	Arms	Adage	Steps	Dances	Mime	Theory	Total
20	10	20	20	20	5	5	100
16	8½	16½	17	B 8½ J 8½	5	5	85

Result—
Honours 85
Passed 65

REMARKS *Very careful + has some good qualities. Rolls ankles. Stretch feet more in bar-work. Improve the carriage in Arabesque.*

Examiner _____

Ballet Examination Result Grade IV

Then came the first of the senior exams, Elementary, in May 1944, during my last year in the primary school.

RIGHT:
Madame Helena Lehmiski, who used to dance at the Gaiety Theatre, London, and now examines for the Royal Academy of Dancing all over the world, shows a class how to do an arabesque in her Birmingham studio.

Madame Lehmiski in the Studio after removal from Station Street

For the senior exams we had to wear the regulation tutu. This had to be made by the recognised dress maker who lived on the other side of Birmingham and Mother and I took the bus over there several times for me to be measured and then to collect this very expensive costume. The bodice was white satin with four flexible, metal "whalebones" inserted into the lining, two front, two back, from just below the bust to the waist. This was to make sure there would be no creases in the bodice. The short skirt had two or three layers of tarlatan, a very stiff, light material, and was overlaid with a fine white net, the whole skirt sticking out stiffly. We had to wear pink tights, without wrinkles and this was universally achieved by having several pennies placed around the hipline inside the tights and, on the outside, being wound round with thin tape around the hips and tied up at the front. These, of course, would be hidden by white frilled knickers. Ballet shoes in pink satin had to be replaced regularly as these soon wore threadbare.

Intermediate Exam: wearing tutus at Madame Lehmiski's

As an eleven year old, I did not consider the expense my mother must have had. She must have scraped every penny to provide me with the necessary outfit.

The Studio School of Dance studios were at the very top of a tall, old building with tall, old buildings on either side, opposite New Street Railway Station. It was not a very salubrious area. We entered the dark, ramshackle old building through tall, wooden, narrow, double doors and then climbed bare wooden stairs, through several landings, up to the fourth floor. We came out opposite the small changing room which had pegs all round the walls for hanging our clothes and a bench seat all round below. Next came Madame's office and then the double doors at the side into the large, bright light of the studio.

On one side of the studio were large windows through which we looked down onto the station and roads down below and out at roof tops on the same level as ourselves. Other walls were covered with huge mirrors from floor to ceiling. They were to enable us to see how we were performing all our exercises. In front of the mirrors were barres. On these we rested our hands while our feet did the movements and we rested our feet for our stretching exercises. In a corner there was a piano.

Through a door on one side was another smaller studio. Madame always taught in the main studio but in this smaller studio reigned her assistant, Miss Wilkins. I dreaded being called in for a lesson to be taken by Miss Wilkins as she was a tartar for correctness and perfection. But could she play the piano! She would sit at the piano in here (yes, there were two pianos), never looking at the notes she was playing but turning sideways on the stool to watch all our movements as she instructed us. And if not looking at us directly, she would be watching us through the mirrors which again covered the walls in this studio. We could never escape her scrutiny. She made us work but, my goodness, how we enjoyed our work when accompanied by that piano. Her fingers on those keys made our feet twinkle and despite being worked to near exhaustion we came out of that studio elated.

It was in May 1944, just before I left the primary school when I was eleven, that I passed the Elementary exam and, as all other students at the same stage have done, I became a member of the R.A.D, the Royal Academy of Dancing.

R.A.D. Membership Card

I now embarked on the work for the Intermediate examination, after which there would be only one more to go, the Advanced, before gaining my teacher's certificate. For this we had extra classes on Saturday mornings. At one, Ruby entered the class in tears and Madame spent time comforting her. Wanting to help, I spoke to her, when she burst into tears again and ran out of the room. I was not looked on favourably as I had upset her again after Madame's kindly words of comfort. It seems she had heard earlier that morning that her brother had been killed in enemy action. Ruby never appeared again.

The end of the war was approaching. Madame Lehmiski and her assistant now decided the time had come to put on a show, the first one since the war began. The venue, The Midland Institute in Birmingham, was booked for two Saturdays, the 14th and the 28th October. This entailed rehearsals and practices during the summer holiday before starting at the Grammar School, at week-ends and in the evenings leading up to the date when the show would be performed. The dances were arranged: they were so imaginative, and the choreography was superb. Parents were asked to help in the making of the costumes and were given all the details for their construction. Some were made for us by people who had made costumes for

Madame's shows before the war. It was amazing how everyone set to to help.

Finally the show date arrived. I was in three dances. The first of these was entitled "When We Were Young" and I took part as one of the school girls. I danced with a hoop, bowling it round the stage. My dress was long and white with lace frills round the skirt. It was my mother's wedding dress cut down to fit. I wore a broad pink sash around my waist. My third appearance was in a folk dance "Tyrolean", dancing with tambourines. My outfit was a white, puff-sleeved, embroidered blouse belonging to my mother, worn under a circular skirt with a front bib. Materials were scarce so Mother's imagination came up with the use of the black-out material which was hung at all the windows to prevent light from shining through. The skirt was trimmed with coloured binding from her work box and yellow flowers cut out from yellow dusters. All the dresses looked so gay as we twirled around, banging and rattling the tambourines.

It was my second dance that was really memorable. The heading was "The Army, Navy and Air Force". The "Army" did their marching sequence. The "Navy" danced the hornpipe, but the "Air Force", which I was in, stole the show. We were all dressed in identical airforce blue colour skirts and jackets and wore the airforce small caps on our heads. After our sequence we formed up in the shape of a plane, some in the "fuselage" (body), four in the "wings" and the one in the front of the plane whirled her arms round and round like propellers while the footlights and the spot light flickered continually. It was a magnificent scene, as though the plane was taking off. The applause was loud and long and it has remained long in the memory.

A
DANCE RECITAL

consisting of

ORIGINAL BALLETS and DIVERTISSEMENTS

By pupils of the

STUDIO SCHOOL OF DANCE,

Principal - HELENA LEHMISKI

Member of Sub-Committee of the Royal Academy of Dancing (Advanced Teachers Certificate). Fellow of Imperial Society of Teacher's Dancing (Operatic Branch). Mem: Cecchetti Society. Advanced Member of International Dancing Masters Association.

Assisted by ELSA WILKINS
Member of the R.A.D. Licentiate of I.S.T.D. (Ballet and Stage Branches) (Hons)
Member of I.S.T.D. (Ballet and Stage Branches) (Hons)

Saturday, October 14th & 28th, 1944
2.30 p.m. in the
LARGE LECTURE THEATRE,
MIDLAND INSTITUTE.

All proceeds to The British Legion.

PART 1.

Musical Moods.

Singers ... Elsa Wilkins and Rita Williams.
Accordionist ... Leonard Rowe.
"Life is Nothing without Music"
Pretty Girls ... S. Leeley, J. Sparks, G. Drew, P. Mason, B. Storey, B. Jones, G. Morgan, J. Thornton, M. Mander, E. Lewis, J. Haworth, E. Appleby at Shirley Thompson.

Chopin Valse ... Lusana Rowe.
"Top Hat" ... Monica Aveyard, June Harding, Eric Spicer and Godfrey Foster.

"Nigger Minstrels" ... Audrey Vann and Brian Richardson, B. Roberts, E. Wych, M. Judson, E. Short, M. Empire, J. Roberts, J. Kenvon with J. Frost.

Alexander's Ragtime Band ... Joan Lee and Leonard Rowe, R. Hill, H. Mac-Pherson, J. Bank, G. Whitton.

"A Lovely Way to Spend an Evening" ... Rita Williams and Rita Williams.

Sea Fever ... Joan Mean.
Her First Love Letter ... Judith Worsnics.
Leaning on a Lamp-post. ... Duncan Bank.
Danse Acrobatique ... Glenys Drew.

Nursery Episode (No. 2.)

Nurse ... Rita Williams.
Gir ... Daisy Jennings.
Boy ... Kathleen Watt.
Golly ... Audrey Vann.
White Cat ... Elsie Watford, Kathleen Brown.
Teddy Bear ... Joan Watson.
Party Doll ... Norma Millery.
Dutch Doll ... Mary Bradley.
Harlequin ... V. Ingha.
Wooden Soldiers ... M. Nevin, V. France, P. Higgins, N. Grayson, S. Bellingham, M. Weodin, L. Mander, M. Chriabey.
Teddy Bears

Polish Mazurka. ... Judith Whittaker, Karl Moss and Joan Morani or Shirley Thompson.
Joy Harding, P. Manton, S. London, G. Drew, J. Seago, E. Sparks, B. Jones, M. Peel.

"No Two Ways About Love" ... Mary Anderson.

Musical Comedy.
"When We Were Young:"
"Blind Man's Bal"

Jolly Dance ... Audrey Vann, with M. Pedmore, M. Pedmore, C. Hall, M. Vine, M. Hill, K. Boyish.
"Tyuma" ... G. Trueman.
Schoolgirls ... Norah Roberts.

Hoop Dance ... Norah Manley and Joan Williams.
Sandals ... Freda-, Sandal, H. MacPherson, D. Hall, A. Yardley.
Needlework ... Mary Boydley, Pat Seal, Mary Anderson, M. Wilson, J. Frost, G. Kenvoy, P. Kohler, J. Marston, E. Short, J. Baker, J. Kowhoue.

"Take it Easy" ... ... S. Thompson or G. Morgan, P. Mason, M. Peel, J. Harwell, Judith Whitaker, G. Drew, E. Speake, J. Harding.

Deep Purple ... ... Joan Morant.

The Army, Navy and Air Force.

Army ... ... Norma Manley and Colin Stowe supported by P. Pearce, K. Williams, K. Wyatt, V. Inglis, B. Poole, A. Larcher, K. Baylis, J. Smith, P. Wood, J. Bamford, P. Higgins, N. Graynoth, M. Navey, F. Brewer.

Navy ... ... Joyce Rawbone and Brian Richardson supported by G. Beasley, M. Wilson, E. Barber, J. Ward, M. Greatrex, B. Matthews, L. Wall, P. Udall, Z. Butler, H. Manners, J. Harris, Y. Yapp.

Air Force ... ... Colin and Anita Moseley supported by D. Hall, G. Slater, D. Smith, J. Baker, C. Thomlinson, M. Viner, N. Leverington, E. Dallison, P. Kohler, J. Waters, J. Marston, A. Yardley.

Egyptian Statuette ... Gladys Morgan.

Swing Shoe Shop ... Brenda Roberts and Margaret Poulton.

Nocturne.

Première Danseuses ... J. Whitaker and J. Morant.

Première Danseur ... Karl Miss.

Coryphées ... ... W. Moakler, M. Peel, J. Harding, S. Lorden.

Corps de Ballet ... ... E. Speake, P. Mason, D. Stanley, G. Drew, J. Lees, B. Jones, S. Thompson.

INTERVAL (10 minutes).

PART II.

Symphony in Black and White.

Duo Dance ... ... J. Harding, M. Peel, G. Morgan, J. Harwell, J. Lees, E. Speake, U. Wilkinson, B. Jones.

Staircase Dance ... ... Gladys Drew.

Valse Acrobatique ... Judith Whitaker.

Helena Trio (2nd) ... Iris and Doris Jeffries, O. Sewell.

Corps de Ballet ... ... G. Beasley, E. Breeze, M. Wilson, J. Rawbone, B. Roberts, M. Padmore, P. Udall, M. Poulton, M. Anderton, H. MacPherson.

Put Your Arms Around Me Colin Stowe.

The Reluctant Milkmaid ... Joan Morant.

Blue Birds in My Belfry ... Dorothy Stanley.

Tyrolean.

Soloist ... ... J. Rawbone.

Girls ... ... J. Harwell, J. Thornton, E. Lewis, A. Yardley.

Boys ... ... J. Manners, B. Fackerell, M. Lane, E. Apperley.

Children ... ... P. Kohler, J. Frost, J. Baker, E. Short, M. Wilson, B. Roberts, M. Poulton, G. Beasley.

Country Fair ... ... Jean Lees and Dorothy Stanley.

"Watch the Birdie" ... Audrey Vanes.

Journey to a Star ... Judith Whitaker.

"Forest Fire"

Fire ... ... J. Morant, S. Lorden, M. Peel, P. Mason, G. Drew, S. Thompson.

Smoke ... ... E. Speake, B. Jones, J. Lees, D. Stanley, J. Harding.

Trees ... ... J. Poole, B. Fackerell, M. Lane, U. Wilkinson, J. Thornton, E. Lewis, S. Sandall, G. Morgan.

When I Sing ... ... Rita Williams.

Bidin' My Time ... ... Jean Lees, Dorothy Stanley, Gordon Banks.

Hunting Dance ... ... Eunice Speake.

Three Girls and a Boy ... J. Whitaker, J. Harding, S. Thompson and Eric Sytee.

Alabama Bound ... ... Rita Williams supported by

Waiting for Choo Choo Special ... ... B. Jones, J. Thornton, E. Apperley, B. Fackerell, J. Poole, R. Hill.

Waiting Passengers ... J. Lees, E. Lewis, U. Wilkinson, S. Sandall, M. Lane, D. Stanley.

Guard ... ... Gordon Banks.

Newspaper Boys ... David Brindley and Harry Fletcher.

Shoe Black ... ... Jean Banks.

Porter ... ... Eric Sytee.

Gay Old Gentlemen ... Leonard Rowe.

Modern Miss ... ... Joan Morant.

Schoolmistress ... ... June Harding.

Children ... ... U. Short, B. Ward, M. Padmore, J. Rawbone, J. Frost, M. Poulton, M. Baguley, B. Roberts.

People from Eastside ... Olive Sewell, Iris and Doris Jeffries.

Midnight Choo-Choo ... Judith Whitaker and Shirley Thompson with M. Peel, M. Kavanagh, P. Mason, D. Neal, G. Morgan, S. Fletcher.

FINALE.

AT THE PIANO . . . . . . ELSA WILKINS

GOD SAVE THE KING.

JOAN MORANT appears by kind permission of DEREK SALBERG.

RITA WILLIAMS by kind permission of JACK HYLTON.

Advanced Members of the R.A.D.

J. MORANT, W. MOAKLER, J. WHITAKER, M. ANDERTON, J. HARDING, E. SPEAKE, S. LORDEN.

Intermediate Members.

G. DREW, B. JONES, D. STANLEY, A. VANES, J. LEES, M. BAGULEY, J. BAKER.

Elementary Members.

SHIRLEY THOMPSON, P. MASON, J. HAYWELL, B. ROBERTS, J. RAWBONE, M. PEEL, S. SANDALL, A. YARDLEY, D. NEAL, S. FLETCHER.

Class or Private Tuition given daily in all branches of Dancing. Coaching for all examinations. The training of children a speciality.

For all particulars apply:—

61, Station Street, or 'phone Mid. 4100.

CHAPTER XIII
Last Dancing Days

I was fortunate to have had piano lessons from a local teacher but, like many children, I did not practise as I should have done. Oh, I loved playing the piano – certain pieces of music that is. My dance exercises were always practised to certain tunes and I enjoyed learning and playing all those, plus several pieces which I found amongst Mother's music in the music stool. She played the piano and would have been very good if she had practised! Like mother, like daughter! Her music teacher, a top-class one, had told her when young, "Don't bother to come to me if you don't practise." She did as he said and did not continue. My special party piece was "In An English Country Garden" and I played that with gusto. But it was not until I was sitting with my son watching him practise on the piano for his first exam that I realised the figuring above the notes on a sheet of music meant something! I had never realised that the '+' indicated that the thumb should play this note. I had always mixed up my fingers as I thought best. No wonder I could not play the piano properly.

The music teacher knew I had dancing lessons and, when in May 1945, VE (Victory in Europe) was declared and everyone wanted to celebrate with street parties, she asked me to join the entertainment and dance IN THE STREET! She said they would move a piano out into the street for me for the accompaniment. Oh dear! At eleven years old I did not have the confidence to do as she asked and said I could not possibly do it. My kind of dancing was not street dancing. I felt I had let her down in her expectations. I cannot remember going to any more piano lessons.

The "Mothers Union" asked if I would dance at their party in the church hall. Now this was totally different as Mother would play the piano there for my accompaniment, so I agreed to dance the dance with the hoop which I had done with the girls in the last show and for which I wore Mother's wedding dress, cut down to size as it was. It was not the same dancing solo to the mothers as it was with the group in the show but it was my effort.

"The Rangers" in our company, the step up in age range from the Girl Guides, planned to put on a show as their part in the celebrations and here also I was asked to dance. In the first scene in which I appeared I had to step out of a picture frame and dance a minuet.

The Rangers' VE Celebration Show

My second turn was the Tyrolean dance with tambourine, again with Mother providing the accompaniment.

Ann on right, in her skirt of blackout material, withyellow flowers made from yellow dusters

In October of this year the Studio School of Dance put on their second show, this time on three Saturdays, 13th, 20th and 27th. Rehearsals took place as usual with extra ones in the evenings and it was on one of these evenings that I became very frightened. Rehearsals went on until quite late in the evenings. We finished around eight o'clock. Normally I would catch a bus close to the studio. We caught our bus from home, the 16A, shortly after it left the terminus and the route went straight through Birmingham and continued across the other side of town to the terminus at Yardley – no connection with our name! During the evening, though, the route was curtailed, our bus stopping at the edge of town and returning to our terminus or going into the bus garage at the end of its shift. Likewise, the Yardley bus stopped at the edge of town on this side. So there was no cross-town service for us from late evening.

It had been arranged that Father would come and pick me up at eight o'clock as the rehearsal finished. The students left the building in twos and threes and I also packed up and left the top floor to come down the four floors in semi-darkness from the deserted studio to wait at the front steps before the narrow wooden doors. Miss Wilkins was the last to leave and, as she passed me, asked if I was all right, and I explained I was waiting for my father to pick me up. There I stood in the dim dingy doorway, my case at my feet, waiting for our car to draw up. I waited. I watched all the men hurrying past to catch trains at the station opposite. There seemed to be no ladies about at all. Here was I, a twelve-year-old girl, standing waiting, trying not to be seen by all the passers-by who must have wondered why a young girl was standing in the shadows. No father arrived. I was becoming frightened thinking I could not stay there all night. I could not catch a bus here. The only way I could get a bus home was to walk across New Street Station with all the unsavoury sights and through town to the bus stop on the other side. I could not do it. I looked at everyone who passed me and decided I would have to ask someone for help. Along came an older, well dressed man with a hat on who looked as though he might help me. So I stopped him. "Excuse me. I'm very frightened. My father has not come to fetch me and I have to walk across the station to get a bus. Could you accompany me please?" It did not occur to me how dangerous it could have been. He looked at his watch. Obviously he had not a lot of time to spare. He agreed he would see me to my bus stop. We hurried along through the dim passageways, through town to my bus stop where he waited with me until my bus came. I thanked him and told him he was so kind. He took out of his brief case a piece of paper and a pen and wrote down his name and address and asked me to give it to my mother.

With relief I ran home from my bus, much to my mother's consternation. What had happened to Father? Of course, his work had held him up and he had finished late so he was very late coming for me. Naturally Mother wrote a letter of sincere thanks to my saviour. What my mother said to my father I do not know! What could have happened to me I dread to think.

The show date arrived and once again the items were so imaginative and the choreography superb. This time I made four appearances. In the opening item, headed "Sophisticated Rhythm", my turn came with five others in "Love is my Reason". The next was appropriate to the wartime, headed "Out of Darkness Comes the Light" with sections called "Peace" (again I was one of six dancers), "War" and "Give Peace in our Time". This was followed by twenty-five dancers filling the stage in

"Corps de Ballet", of which I was one, and last came the most colourful, the most rousing "Evening in the Corral", where I was one of the "Girls". It was all so joyful.

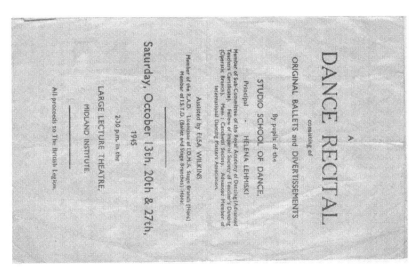

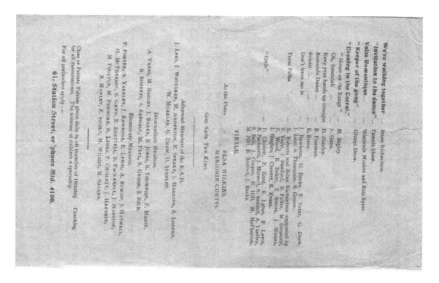

One lesson had been drilled into us: always look as though you are enjoying it and smile. "You must present yourselves to the audience." I think we did.

This advice stood me in good stead. I was no lightweight, no "will-o'-the wisp". The intermediate stage in ballet required me to do point work and this is when I met my Waterloo! Dancing on one's toes is extremely painful and my feet seemed to suffer more than most. We had ruses to help us. We bathed our toes in methylated spirits to harden them. We taped them up with plasters to avoid, and to heal, blisters. We stretched cotton wool over our toes before putting on our point shoes. We poured shellac into the toes of our ballet shoes to harden them, but none of these helped my weak ankles. I needed to practise a lot more and to help me achieve this Father put up a barre in the kitchen for me to work at. I am sorry to say I did not make use of it as often as I should have done. Neither did I put in the necessary ballet practice.

I did practise my tap dances, though. The bus was nearly always empty when I got on as we lived so close to the terminus. I would always aim to sit on the front seat upstairs on the driver's side. From here I had plenty to watch on the long journey to the studio. It also gave me plenty of time to run through my dance routines, to practise what I had not practised at home. While looking through the front window, sitting over the head of the bus driver, my feet would tap away all the sequences until I knew them perfectly without hesitation. I would be able to dance them, in my lesson, as though I had practised for hours. The driver must have wondered what on earth was going on in the upper deck. But I was actively doing my practice oblivious of the noise the continual tapping made above his head.

I was entered in the All England Dancing Competitions in sections for Ballet, Musical Comedy and Tap and on these days I had to have time off school. I was worried about asking for it until I discovered another girl in the year ahead of me was also entered for the competitions and she too had asked for time off. She attended a different dance school from me.

After our performance the entrants in each class were called to the stage to line up for the announcement of the results. All those who had received honours were told to take a step forward when their number was called out. Imagine my surprise when my "Number 2" was called out for the Musical Comedy, my "Number 18" For Ballet and my "Number 40" for Tap, this last being the biggest surprise. For this number my attire was a long-sleeved, white blouse with a big bow at the neckline. It was decided I should wear black "slacks", very few ladies wore trousers, called "slacks" in those days, but Mrs. Madden who lived next door at number 74 did have a pair and said I could borrow them if they fitted. They did. I looked very smart. My number was called. It was my turn to perform. Miss Wilkins played the piano and I began tapping through my routine until suddenly my mind went blank. It had been drilled into us at the shows, if we forgot we did not stand still and look stupid but filled the gaps, dancing steps and smiling. So I tap danced all round the stage, smiling, until the music reminded me of the steps I should be doing. So I finished in style, and was awarded honours!

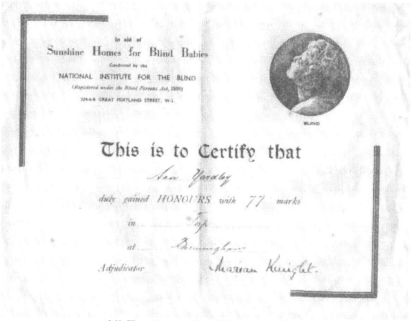

All England Certificate in Tap

I had been attending the Studio School of Dance since returning from the country at the age of ten, having lessons in ballet and later musical comedy – a more relaxed style of dancing – and tap dancing. I had passed my ballet exams up to the intermediate examination. However, after four unsuccessful attempts to pass this intermediate examination, I decided to call it a day and finish dancing. Mother must have been very disappointed after all the money she had spent on my behalf. There had been one occasion when she had been stopped in the road and asked when I was starting my dancing school as her daughter wanted to learn. She would be my first pupil. Mother put the idea forward. How would I like to start my own dancing school? We could hire the hall down the road and she would play the piano for me. But I had no notion of how to go about it. It did not occur to me then to seek advice from Madame Lehmiski. So no! I did not think so. School certificate was looming so I would concentrate on that. But I vowed to myself that I would always do the best I could in whatever I attempted, to make up for Mother's disappointment.

CHAPTER XIV
Holiday and Foggy Days

Victory in Japan – VJ Day – was declared just three months after VE Day. The war was over. However, our lives were still governed by rations and scarcities.

Late one afternoon the phone rang. It was Father. "Pack a case. We're going on holiday tomorrow." Astounded, and in a whirl, Mother asked me to come and help pack a few clothes for Father, herself, Elizabeth and me. "We're going on holiday." What food we had in the house was collected together. Father arrived home very late from work. He had seen in the Birmingham Evening Mail an advertisement for a cottage 'to let' for a week near Pwllheli in North Wales. It was not too far to travel from Birmingham. He phoned through and booked the accommodation and early next morning we set off on our first holiday since before the war started.

Father loved driving and after studying the map the night before he knew exactly where we were heading. We arrived at the small cottage in a lane, miles from anywhere, and were enthusiastically welcomed by Mrs. Hughes. She was Welsh through and through. We were shown into the small dining room. Then into our bedrooms, a small double for Mother and Father and an even smaller double for Elizabeth and me. Then Mrs. Hughes left saying she would be back to cook our evening meal.

The weather was wonderfully warm and sunny this August so we set off to explore our surroundings. We came back for our excellent meal and found Mrs. Hughes was anxious for conversation, lingering in the doorway awhile. We discovered that she removed herself from her cottage to cater for us and went to stay, for the duration of our occupancy, with her younger friend a little further down the lane. Together, they came up to prepare, cook and serve our meals: cooked breakfast and evening meal. They would also prepare sandwiches for us to take out for midday. Was this a new venture for them now the war had ended? They made us very welcome and we had lots of interesting conversations.

Our small bedrooms were very comfortable with little, low windows. The beds were sumptuous with feather mattresses which we sank into with the utmost comfort after a long day out. Mrs. Hughes told us which way to go to the nearest beach and their two girls, Kitty and Toya, who were the same age as we were, accompanied us over fields to a path through a meadow which led down onto the emptiest sandy beach we had ever seen - empty except for the cows. Pentllech beach was heavenly once the cows no longer wanted our company. They left their calling cards which we skirted around before the tide came in to clean the sand. There were warm rocks to lean against when our games of French cricket were exhausted.

Father always joined in with our games, and came into the warm sea with us to swim and splash about. Kitty and Toya often came too. On other days Father drove us to all the nearby deserted little beaches. There seemed to be no-one about but ourselves in the fresh air and open spaces, empty beaches and fields. It was a wonderful holiday taken on the spur of the moment after all the years of war. What concerned Mother most was that she had come away so quickly she had forgotten to bring a coat, but she need not have worried. There was no need for one throughout the entire sunny, hot days we were there. The holiday was so enjoyable that Father booked us in for another one the following year.

This holiday set us up for the winter to come. Whereas the past summer had seemed so warm and sunny, the winter now seemed the worst on record. Snow came with a vengeance, making movement very difficult, but worse than the snow was the fog. All houses had coal fires and therefore chimneys from where the smoke escaped. On mild days the smoke spiralled upwards but on windy, blustery days it would billow this way and that. All the smoke which came out of the chimneys mixed with the moisture in the air, sometimes becoming so thick that the yellow, suffocating air around us was called smog. Scarves were used to cover our mouths to prevent us breathing in the foul air. It was so thick that we could not see a hand in front of us.

Traffic would be at a standstill but buses still tried to get through. Many a time the conductor would leave the bus and walk in front to direct the driver who would be peering through his open windscreen, using the pavement kerbstone to direct his way. Near to our house there was a curve in the main road with three side roads leading off. There were no kerbstones here. The fog was thick. The conductor could not find the way of the road. The driver knew there was a bend in the main road ahead. He over-compensated for the bend and found a kerb which he followed. It directed him down a cul-de-sac, and now the double-decker bus had to get out of that. There were several spectators trying to help, some having left the bus to do so. The driver had to back up the cul-de-sac to the main road with the verbal help of the conductor.

My Father's cousin, Uncle Howard, experienced a very strange journey home during this period. He lived near a tram route. The trams ran on lines down the centre of the road and on one very foggy night he felt the best way to get home would be to follow the tram lines. Trams could still run as their track was assured in any weather, since they automatically ran on the lines in the centre of the road. Peering through his windscreen it was easy enough for Uncle Howard to see the tram lines and follow a tram. He felt he was going very well and would soon be home. The tram stopped, and so did he – in the tram shed!

On one such day the fog was not too thick so Mother, Elizabeth and I set out to walk to Grandfather and Grandmother Yardley's. It was quite a distance but well within our capabilities. We thought we would wait for Father to finish work and come home with him in the car. The weather suddenly deteriorated. The fog thickened. It turned into smog. There was no way we could drive home in this. It was decided we would all have to walk. To our young minds it was an entertaining walk, an adventure, as we could not see a thing in front of us. Father walked close to the pavement-edge kerbstones, having to visualise and use his memory of the layout of the roads we had to cross. I was on the inside of the pavement feeling the way using hedges and walls, calling out when the walls had a break indicating there was a road to be crossed in front of us. The dampness of the air got through to us, making all our clothes very wet. It took very much longer to get home without losing our way than it had taken to get to Grandmother's earlier in the day.

CHAPTER XV
Grandparent's House

Grandmother and Grandfather Yardley now lived in the large house on the corner of the street. All around were back-to-back houses with entries between them. Great-Grandfather Yardley had nine sons, too many for all to live in the family house he had built, so he also bought a house up the next entry to house the older ones.

The family house had space at the side for a yard and, at the back, for stables where horses were kept and it was here in the family home where he started the furniture removing business in 1859 using horse-drawn vans.

Grreat-Grandfather's third son joined him in the business. This was my grandfather, and later my grandfather's two sons (my Uncle Norman and my father) helped run the business. They lived in the family house until they married and from here they continued to run the business exchanging horse power for motor vehicles as the years progressed.

My grandparents lived in this house for the rest of their lives only moving out to Halesowen for a few months during the war when bombs were falling round about. Fortunately their house and the environs escaped the worst of the bombing and that is where I remember them living for several years after the war ended.

Great-Grandfather in his nineties and Ann outside the kitchen
window taken about 1934

Grandfather with horsevan
Yes, the horse is wearing his boots perhaps to avoid skidding
downhill

The horsevan

Sketch of house showing gates with the yard behind.
On the right hand side was the plain brick wall where children loved to chalk
and on the left were the tall gates on rollers which closed off the yard.

Fronting the street at the side of the house were two large, high, wide gates on rollers which could be rolled open or closed to allow horses and vans to pass through. Grandfather and Grandmother Yardley lived here for the rest of their lives.

House very similar to my Grandparents' house, No. 2 Cowper Street

Half way up the street, on the other side, was Holt's Dairy from where the noise of drays being loaded with milk churns, as well as the noise of the dairy itself, could be heard at five o'clock in the morning, as the dairy prepared to set off with their horses on the day's delivery. This noise always awakened us when we stayed at Grandmother's in the large front bedroom, generally around Christmas time, when I was about eleven years old.

Grandfather, the third of the nine sons, took over the business with one of his brothers, Horace, known as Sam, to work for him. Grandfather's sons, my father and his younger brother, my Uncle Norman, then worked in the business. Father had been attending the technical college, training as a draughtsman, but when, in 1912, he was aged fourteen one of the removal men broke his leg. Father was told he must leave the technical college and help with the removal business as they were short handed. Soon horse-drawn vans were replaced by the early petrol-driven vans which Father and Uncle Norman learnt to drive.

A visit to Grandmother's house was so different from being at home. The house was so much older. For a start no-

93

one ever entered by the front door, behind which was a vestibule with a glass door shutting it off from the long hall. The vestibule was where you hung your coat and hat when visiting, and left your umbrella or walking stick in the umbrella stand, before entering the hall. The hall was lit by a gas light. As the gates were always open everyone went up the yard to the back door. Through this door you entered the scullery. Opposite the door was the range which always had a fire burning in the grate to warm the room. It was beside this range that Uncle Horace always sat when he arrived for the day's work. There would always be a large, black kettle of water simmering away on the coals or resting on the hob. On the high shelf over the range there stood something which fascinated me. It was a weather barometer in the shape of an Alpine house. In one open doorway was a man in Tyrolean dress, who always swung forward if it was going to rain. In the other open doorway was a lady dressed in Tyrolean style. If the weather was going to be fine she swung forward. I would stand in front of them for ages waiting for them to move.

In the corner of the scullery was the copper, the huge bowl where washing was done. The water to fill it had first to be ferried from the one cold water tap at the side of the sink or from the kettle, then a fire was lit underneath the copper to heat the water. Along the adjacent side wall was the claw-footed bath, covered over with a board and a cloth. Whenever anyone wanted a bath, usually in the evening, the outside door had to be locked, no admittance, and the inside door to the living room bolted. One never knew when Father or Uncle Norman would be returning from their daily removal job, until the sound of the van was heard entering the yard. All hot water came from the kettle boiling on the range or from the copper which had been prepared hours before to heat the water. Washing up was done in front of the window which looked out onto the yard, in a low, brown, shallow sink with a cold water tap above it on the wall. A small gas oven stood on a cupboard beside the sink. It had two gas rings on the top. It was in this that Grandmother always cooked the Christmas cake which she gave to us as our family Christmas gift. She was rather artistic as the cakes were always iced in white icing with piped stars all around, and on top, in pink icing, she piped a Christmas greeting. But oh! The cakes were so hard that very little of them was ever eaten.

Out of the scullery, into the living room, we passed the long but small narrow pantry where the large, brown bread crock stood on the floor. The dinner plates and large crockery were stacked on the shelf above and on a rail leaning against the opposite wall hung aprons with bibs. Whenever I went to Grandmother's I was given an apron to wear. Slipped over my head it was always long, reaching the floor over my feet, so it was always hoisted up into a pleat at my waist, the straps taken round my back and brought back to the front to tie in a knot.

In the living room was another range where a kettle simmered and food was cooked in the ovens on either side. Both of the ranges always shone with the constant attention of the black lead polish. In front of each was a wide, tall fireguard, the one in the living room being taller and wider than the scullery one, for in here everyone came in to sit on the top and singe their bottoms. The fireguards were about four feet long and stood three-and-a-half feet high with a brass rail on top. They surrounded the whole of the front of the range. At times there were three bodies shuffling along to find the warmest spot. In front, on the floor, they stood on pegged rugs which Grandmother made by cutting up old suits, jackets and trousers and pegging the bits into hessian sacks. She had attempted to make patterns in the brown, blacks and navy blues. She was really quite clever.

Alongside the back wall was the 'sideboard'. What else could I call it? A desk on top was used for the business, with a ledger and a phone beside it and a conglomeration of everything else as well. Drawers underneath had tablecloths, dusters and so on and in the centre was a cupboard in which toys, puzzles and books were kept for children to search amongst.

In the corner was the ceiling-high corner cupboard, the top shelf of which no- one could reach, and below, all the teacups, saucers, jugs and tea pot were kept. The centre of the living room housed the table round which there was hardly room to move. It was always covered with a chenille tablecloth when not laid for meals and under the top, in a drawer, was the cutlery. It was my job always to clean the knives with Vim! No stainless steel cutlery here, no silver. The metal knives were always stained and they waited for my every visit to be scrubbed with a cloth dipped in Vim to bring them up to a shine. That is why my apron waited for me in the pantry. I must always have a job! If I arrived when Grandmother had done the washing I helped her fold the sheets and tablecloths before carrying them out in a wash basket to the nearest stable where the mangle stood. This was a tall, old, heavy mangle with huge, wooden rollers and a large cast-iron handle at the side which was turned to rotate the rollers. I had to guide the folded linen through the rollers so that they came out the other side straight, flat and creaseless for Grandmother to catch them, at the same time turning the handle at the side. Always there was the reminder "Mind your fingers." Oh, crushed fingers were a constant dread!

Mangle

Along the hall was the door to the sitting room and, further on, the door to the "best room" at the front of the house. I do not ever remember seeing either in use, though during the war Father had a billiard table in the sitting room. Opening the living-room door into the hall one noticed a door tucked away in the corner. Inside was a switch for an electric light to light the way down a flight of narrow steps leading to the dark, cold cellar which ran underneath the house. It was here that my grandparents sheltered in the air raids during the war.

The front stairs led up from the hall and had carpet up the centre held in place by frequently polished brass rods. They led up to my Grandparents' bedroom which overlooked the yard. Uncle Norman's room, when he lived at home, was in the centre, over the living room, and then came the large front room which we used on occasions. There was another small bedroom above the side of the living room, over the scullery. It was approached through a hidden door beside the living room range, up the back, carpetless stairs which twisted upwards. This was the room for "Auntie Carrie". It was her domain. She was an old friend, a live-in help. She did wonderful crocheting. One of her jobs was always to polish Uncle Norman's shoes every morning. (Mother always polished Father's shoes every morning too.) The furniture removers always looked smart, wearing a clean, white, calico apron every day. These became so dirty with their work they had to be scrubbed with a scrubbing brush each day before being washed in a tub with the dolly. This was an inverted colander-shaped tool with a long handle to push the clothes up and down in the soapy water in the tub.

Life was hard in those days. My Grandparents had electric light but refused to have electric sockets anywhere. Other than the two ranges and fireplaces in the two unused rooms, there was only a small gas radiator which was lit in the hall only in the coldest weather.

When Mother came to help, as she sometimes did, she "swept" the carpets with a little push sweeper. How she complained at the effort she had to put in after using the easier vacuum cleaner at home. If only Grandmother would consent to having electricity installed it would make their life so much easier. When she offered to iron, this was done using two flat irons alternately heated in front of the grate in the range, and working on the living room table. Of course, she was familiar with this after the time we had spent in the country during the early part of the war.

Grandmother needed a garden. The yard was all blue bricked, so, alongside the high wall of the entry next door, on the fourth side of the yard, a small patch of bricks had been removed for her to have her garden. It must have been all of six feet wide and twelve feet long, a miniscule patch in which she had a central strip of lawn, just wide enough to push a lawn mower along. It had a length of eighteen-inch-high trellis along the front with an arch half way along and a tiny gate. In here she had her prized patch of lilies of the valley and a few annuals from the seeds she planted each year. It was her little bit of greenery. Beside the living room window another couple of bricks had been removed and she was as proud as Punch because a grape seed she had planted had sprouted to provide a vine stem. She always waited each year expectantly for grapes to appear. There was always the twitter of sparrows. Maybe they managed to find bits of hay blown in the wind from the stables, remnants from their use in days gone by.

The furniture vans were always well looked after, with Father doing his own servicing on them. I would watch him filling them up with oil and water. To do this latter chore he would unscrew the special radiator cap of which he was so proud. The vans were Guy vans and radiator caps were moulds of an Indian in his headdress with the words "Feathers in our Cap." This, of course, referred to Guy Motors but I liked to think it meant the excellent service of Yardley's removal firm! The vans were always kept scrupulously clean, being washed down regularly. There was no chance of anyone fingering "clean me" in the dust.

Father's Van showing the radiator cap

Van radiator cap

Scratches were sometimes inevitable as the vans were driven along the roads. The time came when one van needed more than just a wash down. It was taken to the paint shop, then to the sign writers for complete refurbishment. The firm had been established by Great-Grandfather Yardley in 1859. Father went to fetch the new look van which certainly was new look! On close inspection he could hardly believe what he was seeing. The date written on the van was 1958! He let rip! What were they playing at? Could they not read? "We thought there had been a mistake as we considered you were too young to be established in 1859. We thought it should be 1958." It all had to be removed and done again correctly at their expense.

Grandmother was small and slight with her long, grey-tinged-with-yellow hair wound up into a bun in the nape of her neck. She had one affliction: she was stone deaf. Everyone had to shout if she was to understand anything that was said and, of course, she never heard the phone. I went to Grandmother's one morning with Father. The men were all out in the yard attending to the vans except Uncle Horace. He was sitting in the scullery as usual. The phone rang. A removal wanting to be booked? I was mesmerised by what happened next. Uncle Horace, who never ventured further into the house than the scullery, went into the living room, lifted the receiver and shouted into it, "There's no-one here." How I laughed at the incongruity of it!

One thing I enjoyed at Grandmother's was playing with a ball. When the vans were out there was the whole yard where I could play. The house brick wall was tall, wide and windowless on this side of the yard. Nowhere at home could I find such an expanse against which I could throw a ball, aiming higher and higher and catching it before it fell to the ground. I played "sevens" for hours:-

First, throwing the ball against the wall in front of me and catching it,
Second, bouncing the ball on the ground so that it would rise and hit the wall for me to catch it,
Third, throwing the ball against the wall and clapping my hands three times before catching it,
Fourth, lifting a leg and throwing the ball underneath to hit the wall for me to catch it, Fifth, throwing the ball at the wall from behind my back then catching it,
Sixth, throwing the ball at the wall and touching the ground with both hands before catching the ball,
Seventh, throwing the ball against the wall and turning round completely before catching it.

Another game was juggling the balls in the air using both hands then doing two balls with one hand. Next came juggling two balls with two hands, throwing the balls against the wall, then doing the same with one hand. This was followed by juggling two balls against the wall throwing them over-arm instead of under-arm and, as a change, doing the latter two alternately.

It was a treat to have a new ball. We had what we called sorbo rubber balls which bounced very high. To make them go higher still we could slam the ball down hard to the ground. They were tennis-ball size and the more colourful and patterned they were, the more they were prized. Sad was the day when a brand new beautiful bouncer was taken out for its first airing and it was so joyful that it bounced really high, right over a hedge and down into the field below with no chance of coming back to play!

Grandmother's wall was also an excellent place to practise handstands but, before playing any game or performing any acrobatics against this wall, I made sure to roll the huge gates shut as I did not want an audience of the children who lived and played in the street round the corner of the house. They were always playing out here. The whole other side of Grandmother's house was tall, wide, windowless brick and made a marvellous canvas for scribbling on with chalk, unseen by anyone in the house! Grandmother was kept busy going outside every day with a bucket of water and a cloth to remove all these graffiti. If she caught any of the children they had a piece of her mind. They generally disappeared when they heard her approaching. They were the bane of Grandmother's life.

CHAPTER XVI
France

When new pupils started at the Grammar School they were bombarded with all sorts of information, one piece, in the French lessons, being why we should support the Free French. We were asked to donate a small sum each week towards the cause and were issued with a badge to wear on our gymslips. Countries were still at war and the French needed our help. Our French mistress, Miss Evans, organised these collections and, possibly through this association, linked up with a school in Saint Dié, a small town near the Vosges Mountains. The war came to an end in 1945 and in the following year Miss Evans arranged with the French mistress in the school in Saint Dié for the first exchange holiday for students between the schools. And so correspondence began between the pupils in the St. Dié school and in ours. It would improve our French. I would visit my correspondent, Anne-Marie Cuny.

Thoughts turned to what gifts would be suitable to take to our hosts. At this time plastic had just been introduced. Mother thought a gay, brightly coloured, plastic belt would be suitable for Mme. Cuny and for each of her two daughters, Anne-Marie and Françoise.

Three girls in my form said they would like to go, my friends, Margaret, Peggy and me. At 13, I was the youngest of the party. We were put in groups with a senior girl as a leader. Our leader was Doris Juggins whose father had a photographic shop at Lozells, not far from Grandmother's house.

Excitement mounted as the departure date drew nearer. We travelled first by train to Dover and there we caught a boat. We were standing at the rails on the *Prince Albert* watching the cliffs of Dover growing smaller and smaller as they gradually disappeared from sight and we had water all around us. We were heading for Ostend in Belgium and it was a long crossing. In Ostend we transferred to a corridor train which had compartments. It was so very hot and stuffy. The train was stopped for hours along the route. We were tired, hungry and thirsty. Feeling so hot and crumpled I took off my skirt and hung it up from the overhead rack, held in place by my suitcase. As I stood there in my knickers – we did not wear petticoats, now called slips – the compartment door was slid open and in stepped a male railway official. How the girls laughed at my embarrassment.

Oo-la-la!

We arrived in Strasbourg, a journey right across France, and here we were found refreshment in a bare hall with trestle tables on which was a limp salad. We had time in Strasbourg, which is not too far from the German and Belgian borders. Here, I stood in front of the Strasbourg Cathedral clock, fascinated by all the colour and movement which changed every few minutes, showing hours, days, months and seasons.

Another train journey followed taking us to our destination, Saint Dié, which had suffered during the war. My hosts were Monsieur and Madame Cuny who lived outside Saint Dié in the village of Etival-Clairefontaine. My exchange correspondent, with whom I had exchanged a few letters, was Anne-Marie who seemed so much older than me, about eighteen I thought though I suppose she was not quite that old, perhaps around seventeen. Her sister, Françoise, would have been two years younger and their brother, Jean, nearer my age, about fourteen. He was not interested in a thirteen-year-old English girl with plaits! A pretty girl with fair curly hair came to visit and they spent time laughing and teasing each other. I rarely saw Jean.

My hosts, the Cuny family

After an exhausting journey and a welcome night's sleep I was awakened very early in the morning by the sun streaming through the bedroom window. Getting out of bed to look out on the scene I was amazed to see the whole family attending to the rows of beans on sticks standing above the baked soil. No flower, no grass to be seen. I said how surprised I was to see everyone out so very early, before 6.00 a.m., and it was explained to me that work had to be done before the day became too hot.

The back view of the house at Etival-Clairefontaine -
My bedroom window on the left

When it came to our evening meal I commented on the beautifully painted dinner plates, each one different, bearing a colourful arrangement of fruits. I was surprised to find the meat with gravy was served alone on the plates. Bread was served too. When the meat was eaten, the bread was eaten after it had been used to wipe up the gravy, leaving the plate clean for the next course to be served – the vegetables. I definitely liked the small narrow beans cooked whole. They seem to have been cooked in oil and tasted very different to any I had had before. They must have been freshly picked from their 'patch'. I could not call it a garden. I liked their bread – a stick of yellow! It must have been made from maize. As at all French tables, the meal was accompanied by wine – red wine – not as we would have had in England. It was more like a cordial and would certainly not have made me tiddly!

Mother had suggested I could help Mme. Cuny where possible. I was used to ironing – my Guide uniform – so I offered to do the ironing for her. After watching me first of all she decided I was a competent little helper and in this way I chatted to her in my expanding French. I told her I rode a bicycle back at home. They had bicycles she said, which I could ride if I wished. I was in my element. Out came the bicycle and she took a long time to explain something about the wheels and the pedals which I did not quite understand but nodded my head up and down as if

I understood. I soon found out what the lengthy explanation had been about! Off I went on a short ride round the lanes. There was no traffic at all. The brakes seemed a little weak but I would go steady pedalling along the flat road. I suddenly found myself stopping. I pedalled off again, then found I was stopping again. It was quite worrying until, after starting off again, I discovered if I pedalled backwards, brakes were applied to the wheels. So that was what the instructions had been about. I had not come across this braking system before. Later that day I said I would go for another ride and went as far as the next village, all very flat and no hills. As one must in France, I rode on the right-hand side of the road, happy as a lark, so happy indeed that I rode the whole way back without holding the handlebars at all, pedalling away, forwards that is, not backwards, all the way no-handed.

It was decided a bicycle expedition would be a good idea and we would take a picnic. Anne-Marie, Françoise, a friend, Bernadette, and I set off and were soon joined by Anne-Marie's boyfriend, Marceau, but we must not mention that he came along too!

Anne-Marie and Marceau

With Bernadette in the centre her friend on her right and me wearing a dress made at school and with plaits framing my face

On a bench at cemetery where we stopped for a rest

Mme. packed our lunch in two haversacks and I asked to carry one on my back, helpful as I must be. We had not gone far when it was noticed there was gravy seeping out of my haversack and down the back of my dress. What must we do but turn back so that I could change my dress and sort out the haversack. The gravy had leaked out of the container, but it is something we at home would never have thought of taking.

Anne-Marie, Françoise and Jean in their garden

One morning Anne-Marie said she would take me to show me where her father walks. Her father was a straight up and down man, rather severe looking, and wore a shirt with sleeves rolled up, trousers with a belt – a working man. I wondered where he walked and how far? It seemed strange. We cycled till we came to what seemed like a large garage and through the open door I saw loads of planks of wood. I did not quite realise it must have been a saw mill. M. Cuny showed us round. I wondered where he walked. Ah! It dawned on me. Anne-Marie's accent! We went to see where her father WORKED. I set to to explain to Anne-Marie the English pronunciation and the difference between WALK and WORK.

It was a very hot day – as they all were during that visit - when Anne-Marie, Françoise and I set off on our bikes once again to an orchard which they owned. Here were the most delicious plums which we had come to pick. They were large and so juicy, just saying "Eat Me" which I did. We stayed picking the baskets of fruit quite a while in the hot sun. We had no hats on our heads and I suffered the consequences. I was sick. Was it the plums or was it sunstroke? Mme. Cuny knew how to cure it. She sat me on a stool in the kitchen. The iron was heated. I removed my clothing and she placed a sheet of brown paper on my back over which she ironed me! Back and forth, up and down my back she ironed me – Oh, it was so comforting and a marvellous cure. I was soon right as rain.

Anne-Marie had to visit an elderly friend of her mother's to deliver a parcel. Would I like to accompany her? As it involved a bike ride I was delighted to go and as she disappeared inside the house I said I would stay and wait outside. There was a pile of tree trunks, perhaps awaiting collection for the saw mill, which had caught my eye, a lovely place to try climbing and clambering over them. While I was doing this I heard a voice call, "Hello Girl". Wondering where it was coming from I turned and met an elderly lady – elderly to my mind but possibly only about forty – coming toward me from the house. Anne-Marie must have told her I was waiting outside. Oh! Someone spoke English! So for a few minutes we enjoyed our conversation before it was time for me to leave.

On another day I was taken to a fair – a market – and we came upon a sweet stall. Sweets were scarce in England, still only bought with coupons in our ration books. The sweets looked so attractive I decided which to buy and was amazed to find that sweets were bought separately. So I bought my one toffee!

There were other stalls there which caught my eye and here I bought my gifts to take back home. I chose a hand-crafted, round, wooden pot with a picture of St. Dié painted on the front. It could be used to hold spills for lighting the fire or for smokers to light their cigarettes, Father being one of these. This was for Mother. For my father I had already bought a model of the boat we were on, the "Prince Albert".

Round wooden pot

I bought a small, round, flattish wooden dish with a lid studded with brass buttons and the words St. Dié written on it which I kept as my own souvenir.

Wooden dish

For Elizabeth I found a hand-sized little doll.

Elizabeth's doll

Monsieur Cuny took a day off work and took us in the car for a long drive to a lake, Lake Gerardmer, a day which was so enjoyed. But on arriving back at the house the weather had changed, becoming hot and oppressive. As it grew dark the rain came then the lightning. It was a spectacular lightning display which lit up the rooms as if it were daylight. I retreated into the room away from the door and window, very scared and frightened at the intensity of the storm. But Françoise was drawn to the spectacle and opened wide the front door, standing there watching all the fireworks and the wind lashing the trees. It seemed to go on for ages. She was asked, requested, encouraged to come back inside, away from the door but resisted all our entreaties until the violent storm abated.

Front of house at Etival-Clairefontaine

The time came to return home after a memorable stay with the Cuny family. To remind me of my stay with them Anne-Marie, Françoise and Jean all drew and painted beautifully in my autograph book. Mme. Cuny told me my accent when speaking French was very good. I felt my visit to France had been successful.

Before leaving, Mme. Cuny packed a sandwich for my journey. She had put in slices of the yellow stick bread and, very kindly, a square of chocolate to eat with it.

Our experiences were exchanged on our long journey home and we arrived back in Birmingham late in the evening. As my family were away on holiday, it had been arranged that Uncle Norman would pick me up at the station and take me back to Grandmother's house for the night. The next morning he would see me onto the train to Wrexham where my family were to meet me and we would all return to the cottage for the rest of their holiday.

As the girls gradually disappeared along with their luggage and the parents who had come to collect them, I stood waiting for Uncle Norman. Doris, my group leader, waited with me, as did her father who had come to collect her. We waited until we were the only ones left and still no Uncle Norman arrived. Suppose he had forgotten! Doris' father said he would take me to Grandmother's which was not far from where he lived. By now it was dark. There were no lights to be seen at Grandmother's house. The tall gates had been shut and bolted. The only thing we could do would be to bang on the front door, which we did and brought the police onto the scene. It was impossible to get any response. Grandmother was stone deaf, Grandfather would not hear either from their bedroom in the centre of the house. The banging on the front door, which was never opened, would not be heard through the closed door of the vestibule behind it. The only bedroom windows, apart from the front where we occasionally slept, overlooked the yard which was now enclosed behind the locked gates. So Doris' father said the only thing to do was for me to go home with them for the night and they would bring me back in the morning.

Uncle Norman had indeed forgotten me. I did get on the train to Wrexham where the family was awaiting me ready to hear more tales than they expected to hear.

CHAPTER XVII

Correspondents

Back from my visit to France I found awaiting me letters from around the world, for among the bombardment of information we received when starting at the Grammar School had been a leaflet asking for students who wished to correspond with boys and girls in other countries. "Please tick the boxes of countries in which you are interested." So I ticked boxes here, there and everywhere!

I then started correspondence with June in Australia, which did not last very long, but, to remember her by I still have a wooden egg cup made in one piece from Australian wood. In France I exchanged letters with Denise, which lasted a year or two. We exchanged gifts, one of which was a writing box with fretwork all over it, including my name worked into the pattern, and a press stud to fasten it, to close the lid, made especially for me. I remember knitting a pair of mittens for her in red, white and blue, very patriotic. An older girl from Switzerland wrote to me and sent her photograph which showed her plaits. They were longer and thicker than mine, but our correspondence did not last long. A letter came from Hans in Holland but that petered out as we had nothing in common.

I had two letters from girls in the same school in Ohio, U.S.A. Shirley discontinued writing but Ann has been a constant penfriend for almost seventy years. When our families were younger our paper chat became an annual, very long letter, but as they have grown older we now exchange letters more often, nearly always accompanied by photographs. Ann has been to visit me, and with my younger sister, Jane, I returned the visit to Ohio. We had wonderful times. We now exchange news of our grandchildren and great-grandchildren.

CHAPTER XVIII
Uncle Howard and Near Disaster

I always enjoyed a visit from Uncle Howard, Father's cousin, Auntie Miriam and their daughter, our cousin, Carol. Carol was a little younger than Elizabeth. The pair of them would disappear to do their own thing. Uncle Howard and Father would gravitate to the lounge and, sitting by the fire, would discuss manly business. Uncle Howard was a pattern maker with his own workshop where he worked in wood. He had made patterns for components used in the Cunard shipping line. Auntie Miriam and Mother stayed as always in the kitchen, the most popular room in the house, and it was from here that laughter always erupted. Auntie Miriam could see the funny side of every situation and was very entertaining indeed. What happened to me? I would creep into the kitchen and sit quietly on the stool up in the corner by the stove trying to be as invisible as possible, listening intently to all the cross-chatter.

It was Auntie Miriam who told us of Uncle's following a tram and the tram rails to guide him home in the thick smog only to find when the tram stopped that he was unaware that he had followed it into the tram shed. She related the time she had to wash his brown coat-overall. In his workshop where there was always dust and sawdust, he always wore a brown coat-overall to cover his clothes. As she prepared it for washing she felt something hard in the material and discovered a long tack, the sort used to knock wood together. He had accidentally torn his overall so he had fastened the tear together with a large tack. In my imagination I saw him with his overall on the work bench hammering the tack into the join as he would with wood, but, of course, this would not solve his problem as the overall would be pinned to the work bench. Inwardly I gave a giggle! Auntie Miriam saw the funny side of this too. He had used the tack as a very long pin – his version of a repair.

It was just after the war had ended and they had planned a week-end away but, as usual, they were late leaving. Auntie Miriam had always to make sure there were no dirty clothes left at home and insisted on washing everything clean before they left. So they were late and it was getting dark. On the way Uncle

Howard had to stop at a garage for petrol. Having filled up he set off again with his collie dog, Dell, in the front beside him since Auntie Miriam and Carol had chosen to be in the back so they could sleep. Dell was a little agitated at first but a few gentle words settled her down. All was quiet for many miles. In the back they seemed to have dropped off to sleep. Uncle Howard spoke to them but was unanswered. A little further on he spoke to them again. No answer. He tried to feel behind him whilst driving but his arms would not reach far enough to wake them, so he pulled up and stopped. There was no-one there! He had been driving many miles all alone. When he had stopped for petrol Auntie Miriam had seen something in a shop window and she and Carol had got out of the car to have a look leaving Uncle Howard to depart, not realising they were not in the car. Oh, what were they to do – miles from home? The garage owner sympathised with them saying, "Not to worry. He will be back again very soon for you when he realises you are not with him." "Oh no, he won't, you know," said Auntie Miriam. "He won't know we're not there. He'll just keep going." The garage owner was astounded to hear this. They were offered refuge in the petrol station until Uncle returned very much later. As for Uncle Howard, when he discovered his lack of passengers, he just had to retrace his steps to find them. It is no wonder Dell was agitated. She knew there was something wrong. In the telling Auntie Miriam could laugh at the preposterous situation of her husband driving away without knowing he had left them behind, that they were not in the car. Just like him! Both parties had something to answer for!

We had enjoyed our holidays in Wales so much after the war had ended that, having heard about them, Uncle Howard expressed a desire to join us with his family. So it was arranged that they would come with us to the cottage for a week's holiday. The cottage was some distance on past Pwllheli. We were all to travel together, Uncle Howard in his car, while we would be in ours. To me it was great fun to see us together as both cars were alike: Morris 10, green and black, with number plates almost consecutive. Ours was AAC 656 and I thought the cars looked like twins. The time of departure was arranged. We waited for them to come, but as time passed and Father became more and more vexed and impatient with their late arrival he phoned them to say that we were leaving and they would have to follow. He had already given them all necessary instructions and directions. All went well for Uncle Howard until he reached Pwllheli where he had to ask a policeman for further directions. This created quite a problem as Uncle Howard's pronunciation of the Welsh language did not quite tally with the policeman's, added to which he did not know the actual address, just "something Sarne". Now there are two areas past Pwellheli with "Sarne" in their name. The policeman asked which one Uncle wanted and Uncle did not know, but that he was going to Mrs. Hughes – as if there was not a "Mrs. Hughes" everywhere in Wales! After much gesticulation and frustration a direction was sorted out, which proved to be the right one, and they arrived to find us waving them in the right direction, wondering what had happened to delay them so long. We were entertained to a long, very funny, explanation of course from Auntie Miriam.

Back row: Elizabeth, Father, Uncle Howard,
Middle row: Mother,
Front row: Auntie Miriam with collie dog, Dell,
Auntie Gertie and Uncle Norman who were visiting us,
Carol in the very front.
I took this one.

Uncle Norman took this one with me on the back row.

That week passed with great enjoyment until we arrived at the beach. This was a long, wide, flat, firm, sandy beach on which cars could park and was ideal for playing games of cricket and other beach activities. There were warm, sun-baked rocks where we could lean our backs and enjoy our picnic.

Father had bought for us a blow-up dinghy. It had two oars with which we could paddle it along. After using the car pump to blow it up it was ready to be launched. Mother was not enamoured of it. She stayed at the rocks. Father had attached a long rope to the dinghy for safety reasons as he did not want it to drift too far away and the rope was tied round a rock to secure it. Mother was to sit and watch while we venturesome folk pushed and paddled around the dinghy before climbing aboard. We were in our swimming costumes while Father and Uncle Howard had rolled up their trouser legs.

Mother waved to us and we waved back. It was great fun. Mother continued to wave and we returned the greeting. After a while Mother's waving became more energetic so we waved vigorously. We were having a great time. Then we could see Mother beckoning more vigorously still. We decided she thought it time for us to come in and reluctantly we paddled the dinghy back. We seemed to be a little further out than we thought. Going in close to Mother we realized the rope had left the rocks and had floated around behind us. As the beach was so flat the incoming tide swiftly reached Mother, but not only Mother! She was trying to call us in to tell us the sea was fast approaching the cars. By the time we had reached her and pulled the dinghy ashore, the tide was lapping the front wheels of the cars which were standing side by side.

The men's faces went white. As we watched, the water rose higher and higher, now half way up the wheel hubs, now washing the running boards below the doors. Uncle Howard quickly took off his trousers and put them on the roof of his car. He opened the car door, put the key in and started the engine. He put his foot on the accelerator hard to get the car moving out of the sand and the wheels immediately sank down deeper into the sand. The harder he pressed the accelerator the deeper into the sand went the car. A by-stander was delighted to tell us they had lost a Rolls Royce in the sand like that last week. Another by-stander was more helpful and said he would fetch the farmer's tractor, kept at the top of the beach to give us a tow out and very quickly the tractor appeared. Obviously, they were aware of rescues about to be needed. A tow rope was fitted to Uncle's car. The tractor started up and tugged the tow rope. It broke. Very quickly a chain was found and fitted and, as the water was rising higher and higher, the tractor just managed to pull the car out. The tractor continued to pull the car along the beach with water spluttering and spitting out of the exhaust pipe. The tractor carried on along the beach well away from the incoming tide. Then, with a sudden shriek, Uncle was running as fast as he could in his underpants after his car, trying to catch up with it shouting "Stop, Stop! My trousers!" There they were on the roof of his car travelling away from him behind a tractor way up the beach.

Stop! My trousers!

At the same time as all this was happening Father had witnessed Uncle's endeavours. He got into his car but refrained from putting as much pressure on the accelerator, consequently the car did not sink as deeply into the sand and he was able, very tentatively, to ease it out. He was able to reverse up the beach from the water's edge. "We've lost many cars like that down here," was not the most helpful comment while Father's and Uncle's faces were drained of all colour. A near catastrophe – a near disaster.

Eventually, with the hot weather which continued for the rest of the holiday, and plenty of time spent on cleaning up, the cars dried out, never to venture onto that beach again. The thought of what could have happened made everyone shudder but the tale was told for many years afterwards, with much laughter, of Uncle Howard chasing up the beach in his underpants after his trousers.

CHAPTER XIX
Mixed Company

My journeys to and from school on my bike coincided with the special bus service which ran for the pupils at the High School. This school bus was nearly always driven by the same, very smart young driver, dubbed "the Duke" and he got so used to seeing me on my bike that he would wave as he passed. I even started to wait for his bus to come as I joined the main road from the back lane to the school. This was fun and made my journeys to and from school far more exciting. I began to work out other times when he was on our route and, when going to town, would time my arrival at our bus stop to get on his bus. The best seat was inside at the front behind the driver and when I would catch his eye in the mirror he would give me a wink. I had a crush! He made my day when I was sitting up on the top deck and at the end of his shift he came up and sat on the seat beside me. He said he was going back home to Bridgend in Wales. Crush over! No more waves and winks to look forward to.

On arriving home, thoughts had to turn to homework and I discovered it was best to get it done as soon as possible after arriving home. Often Mother would have tea ready for us. In those days we had breakfast before we left for school, dinner at midday and tea at 'tea-time' with a little 'something' such as biscuits or cake and a drink of milk or cocoa for supper before bedtime. There was no thought of a cooked meal in the evening. Mother would have the tea trolley laid with a tray cloth on which would be waiting plates, cups and saucers (mugs were not used then, the only ones we had being enamel ones which we used in Guides) teapot, milk jug and sugar basin. A plate of food would be waiting for us hungry folk: watercress or fish-paste sandwiches, maybe a plate of hot toast or pikelets (now called crumpets) and some of her home-made cake to finish with. We drank tea always with a spoon of sugar, and milk, never coffee as we know it today. All we had then was Camp Coffee, a liquid mix which came in a bottle, a spoon of which was put in a cup of hot milk and was supposed to taste like coffee.

In the evenings, apart from Girl Guides and our Busy Bee meetings, I would go to the Youth Club which had been organised by Mr. Barnsley, one of the parents. This was a new conception. The Club met in the Church Hall on Tuesday evenings for all the young folk on the estate. Here we could do organised craft work, or play table tennis, which was not new to me as we had a table tennis table at home. It had been made to fit on the dining room table and was hinged across the middle. One half of this had been used as the 'black out' which had perfectly fitted the large window of the cottage where we lived at the beginning of the war. Now we could play table tennis in our dining room with just enough room to move sideways between the table and the sideboard at one end and between the table and the window at the other end, but what did that matter? There was a little more room at the sides. We enjoyed hitting the ball over the net as fast as we could. Father played with us and occasionally Michael from next door came in for a game and he could slam the ball harder than ever I could. Down at the hall it was a different game, there was room to move about. We were far more athletic down there.

Around this time the Curate at St. Mary's suggested a group of us could run our own church service on a Sunday morning before the main service. He felt that a service for teenagers would attract more young people to Church. We were mostly at the Grammar School or High School, and there were about ten of us who started the service. Freda, Joy, a girl who lived near to us, and I went. It was to be known as 'Knighthood'.

Freda and Ann

We had two or three hymns which were accompanied by one of the group on the piano positioned at the top of the nave beneath the bell tower. We all took it in turns to take the service. One chose the hymns, one read the collect for the day, one gave the talk and one said the prayers, and these were organised on a rota system. Several of those present, boys and girls, went to the High School. I was rather in awe of them. They were so much cleverer and more sophisticated than I was and could give the talk without reading from notes. I hated this task and when my turn came I read a biblical story. I was happy to take the service, announce the hymns and read my chosen prayers when my time came. Occasionally Bishop Linton, who was head of our Church, would come in and listen. The service was over when the bell ringers could be heard climbing the steps up to the bell tower and beginning to ring up the bells, all eight of them, which boomed over our heads, calling the worshippers to the eleven o'clock service. We would all drift our way home in twos and threes. I was once invited to one of the High School girl's Christmas parties to which some of the Knighthood group went and remember playing 'sardines', a kind of hide and seek, and hiding in a wardrobe waiting to be found. I was never found!

No, our spiritual needs were not neglected. Mother was confirmed into the Church of England as an adult, being encouraged by the membership of Mothers' Union which she had helped found on our estate. She suggested I should be confirmed too. This was when I was thirteen. Following tradition, we girls wore white dresses for the confirmation ceremony but, as I did not have one, I was able to borrow from one of the church ladies who kept a wardrobe for this purpose. I went to be given a suitable dress but, as I was one of the last to arrive, most of the choice had gone. I was issued with a dress which fitted but it was minus the belt which had gone missing. When the day came for the confirmation in our church, St. Mary's, by our own Bishop Linton, I remained at the back of the queue, not wanting to be seen as the girl in a dress without a belt. I felt so uncomfortable. I had always been so precise and it mattered to me that I was not properly dressed. Did anyone else notice? No, but it is these insignificant situations which remain in my memory.

It was now that the long summer evenings seemed to go on for ever. After homework, and at week-ends, some of us would go down to the railway, this side of the park, where there was an open patch of ground. We would congregate down there, leaving our bikes against the railings beside the railway. I would always have a ball with me and we would practise throwing and catching. But there was another activity too – collecting train numbers. Many of the steam trains coming through the park had names and we all had little books in which the names and numbers of the different classes of engines were printed. Every train seen would have its name and number underlined in our little books and the object would be to see and mark off as many as possible in each class. So, when a train came through, there would be a mad rush to the railings to 'cop it'. There would be shouts of 'Did you get it?' and "What was it?"

There was one boy who always stood at the railings beside his bike but never joined in any of our games.

"Orange Bike"

He was a High School boy. I had often seen him racing past our house on his orange bike and disappearing down the lane. I wondered where he was going in such a hurry and why, until I noticed him down at the railway beside the railings up by the signal box. The signal man was used to seeing him there watching and logging all the trains and he would often lean out of the signal box window and chat with him. I would watch from a distance. One day I noticed his bike was there but he was not. He had been invited into the signal box. The signal man noticed that I was often there and one day, when I was watching, he asked me if I would like to go into the signal box too. There I discovered that the boy with the orange bike often worked the signal box under direction from the signal man, pulling levers to change the signals and tapping messages on the bells. He was in his element. I stayed there quite a while asking questions and watching until I realized how late it was getting, whereupon I reluctantly left the box and the occupants to return home, riding my bike up the lane as if in a dream.

CHAPTER XX
Vanity

I had had plaits for ever! Mother had said I should give my long hair a hundred strokes of the brush each day. She always commented on the burnished shades which appeared in it. I am sure she looked for resemblances to her father in my colouring for he was ginger through and through with freckles everywhere. I did not want to be called "Ginger". It brought back memories of one of the girls who came to the country school where I was evacuated. She was one of the gypsy girls. The gypsies travelled around the country doing casual labour such as fruit and hop picking and their children had to attend the local school. They did not integrate very well as they were there for so short a time. This girl, only about nine years old, had very ginger hair and we all called after her "Carrots", which of course she did not like.

My plaits were styled in different ways beginning with two down my back from an early age. I must have been about five. My Godmother, Mother's friend who we called Auntie Cis, was living with us at the time and was a help in looking after Elizabeth in that she sat with her making sure she did not cry which would affect her recovery after her operations. She was only eighteen months old. All was quiet. Mother wondered where I was. She searched for me all over the house then called for me in the garden. Nowhere was I to be seen. I was in Auntie Cis's bedroom. I had been having a good look round. Mother found me sitting on the floor by the window beside Auntie Cis's bed. It was not till we went out onto the landing that she found her daughter was one plait less. I had found a pair of scissors. Looking round and finding nothing on hand suitable for cutting, my plaits fell into my eye line and what better than to use the scissors to snip away at that. Holding my plait in my hand I wondered what to do with it. I pushed it down behind the bedside cupboard which is where Mother found it. So two 'bunches' had to do for a while.

I had two long plaits down my back, the sort boys sitting behind liked to dip into ink wells. I folded them up and tied them up with ribbons.

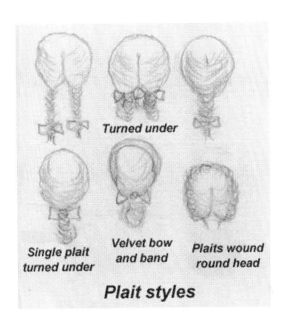

Turned under

Single plait turned under | **Velvet bow and band** | **Plaits wound round head**

Plait styles

I had one plait and folded that one up and tied it up with a ribbon. I did the same, this time having a velvet bow which I snapped around it with a matching velvet bandeau over my head. I also had two plaits taken up to pin (or grip) over the top of my head, framing my face. But just now I wanted something different. When we were at the cottage during the war Mother had dressed my hair differently. She changed my plaits to ringlets. How one suffers to be beautiful! It required me to have my hair wrapped around rags and in this style I had to sleep overnight. She would tear up strips of cotton at least twelve inches long and half an inch wide. My hair would be gathered in strands and, while I held one end of a strip of cotton, she would take the rest over my head and wind it around a small handful of strands of hair. When the 'twist' reached the end of the hair and cotton strip I had to hold it while she took the end I had been holding and wound it round on top of the previous 'twist'. When it reached the bottom the cotton ends were tied in a fairly tight knot so that it would not come undone. This was repeated all round my head until there was no hair left to bind and I looked like 'Topsy'. I slept on all these bundles of hair and rags and the next morning when they were unwound I would have lovely ringlets.

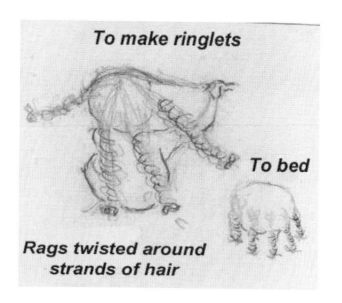

To make ringlets

To bed

Rags twisted around strands of hair

Now was the time to relinquish plaits in favour of ringlets and I knew I could do this myself. The method was the same but instead of me holding the end in my hand my teeth came in handy. Instead of Mother doing the twisting I could do it myself, and I could grab the cotton end in my teeth. Vanity comes before a fall! The next day I was so anxious to get down to the railway that I quickly got ready and whisked my bike out of the garage to hurry down the lane. I had not gone far before my hair felt different. There, at the back, was a 'Topsy' in rags! In my haste I had overlooked one rag-twisted strand of hair. Oh the mortification if I had arrived before discovering my predicament! I immediately turned tail to race home and remedy what I had overlooked, before leaving the house once again in my new hair style – my ringlets. I have recently discovered, in a couple of old photographs, that Mother also had her hair in ringlets fashioned by her Mother. So that was where the idea came from!

Grandmother and Mother with ringlets

CHAPTER XXI
A New Addition

I often helped Mother around the house. On fine days I liked to be out of doors and enjoyed being in the garden. Outside the dining room French window and along the back of the house was a raised crazy paving terrace which Father had built after arriving at this new house. Weeds grew in between the oddly shaped pieces of flag stones and I always enjoyed cleaning them out, deriving great pleasure and satisfaction in seeing a cleaned up area. Of course I could not do it all in one go, it kept me occupied for several days.

We had two lawns, one front and one back. In olden days a scythe would cut the grass but now we had progressed to a push mower, ages before petrol or electric mowers were in common use. It was hard work, especially if the grass had been allowed to grow long. Mother had the job of cutting the lawns and she did get so hot doing it. She asked me to trim the edges afterwards to make them look smart and I did this with shears. How my arms ached! Sometimes I would take it into my head to sweep out the garage and was well satisfied with the end result after my effort.

Mother asked me to dust in the dining room making sure not to forget the chair legs and the table legs. All this was good training for a future housewife. I was asked to shop at the shops round the corner and she would tell me what meat to buy at the butchers. I always asked for a lean piece of beef; I always said to the butcher, "And a piece of fat to cook it, please."

Mother did not go out much as she had a lot to do in the house but would always take a little stroll up the road in the evening. And then we found we were to have an addition in the family. Mother must have told me because I remember going to school and telling my friends where upon Peggy, who was with me on the visit to France, said that her mother too was expecting a baby. If this were to happen in the evening we would go up the road to Mrs. Sargent, the widow who lived at number 62, where we would stay the night. It was Tuesday. I had just returned from the youth club and, arriving at the front door, Father opened it and said "Not tonight, thank you! You are up at Mrs. Sargent's. Elizabeth has gone already." It was November 25th. Early on the morning of November 26th, before we went to school, both Elizabeth and I went in to see Mother and our new baby sister. Mother was in bed looking very pale. She had had a haemorrhage, whatever that was! She would be in bed for a while. In those days it was normal for new mothers to spend two weeks in bed to recover from the birth and gradually return to normal. In due course Peggy had a baby sister. Diana, and we had baby Jane.

A 'home help' had been engaged to come at 8.00 a.m. before we left for school and stay until 4.00 p.m. when we returned. Mrs. Cavanagh was a small, plump, happy person and I remember her for one thing. She cooked the most marvellous chips. She would half cook them in the chip pan, then put them aside on a plate, they would then be returned to the chip pan for final cooking. They were soft inside and deliciously crisp and crunchy on the outside.

We asked Mother what she was going to call our new sister. "Mary Jane". "Oh no! You can't call her Mary Jane," said I. "All the children will chant:-

> "Mary Jane, Mary Jane,
> Where do you live?
> Down the lane.
> What's your number?
> Cucumber."

She will hate it!" So it was turned round to Jane Mary.

CHAPTER XXII
A Very Nice Mistake

Near to us was another big park, Handsworth Park, next to St. Mary's Church. Every year they held a marvellous flower show, second only to the one held at Shrewsbury. These were the two outstanding shows of the year. This park was large with laid out beds and borders and paths everywhere along which to meander. It had a lake, on which we could take out rowing boats, and lots of wild fowl round the perimeter. A very ornate bandstand was in the centre of the park where a band would play and entertain on Sunday afternoons. On the far side of the park were tennis courts where, later on, Father and I would go early on a fine Sunday morning to play tennis in our fashion. There was a bowling green and a small café. Here on fine days Mother would push Jane in the pram, have a cup of tea and a rest, before returning home through this lovely park.

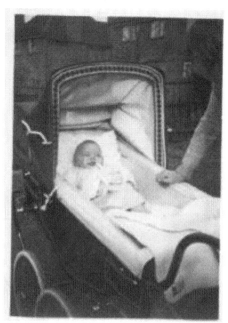

Jane in the pram

It was the place to walk on Sunday afternoons and on one Sunday, as I was pushing baby Jane round in the pram, I found myself accompanied by the boy on the orange bike. He walked with me, helping to push the pram. I was fifteen.

It was a few months later when I told Mother that I would take Jane to see Auntie Cis who had now moved to Stockland Green on the Outer Circle bus route. I carried baby Jane to the number 11 bus stop where Elizabeth had always got on the bus to go to school, and when it came it was full. However, I got on and immediately a very polite, elderly gentleman stood up and said "Have my seat luv, sit here with your babby." I did thank him and I did sit down but I blushed to the roots of my hair wanting to shout out "She's not MY BABY. She's my sister!" In those days young girls with babies were classed as unmarried mothers who had misbehaved. It was a stigma. Why, at the top of Worlds End Road there was a large Victorian house where such girls went to have their babies before having them adopted. How different is society nowadays. In later years Mother told Jane she was a mistake, but a very nice one though!

And so began our life with Baby Jane.

Ann and Elizabeth with baby Jane

Ann, Elizabeth and Jane

CHAPTER XXIII
Lindy Lou

It was around this time that Father brought home a dog. A lady dog, named Lindy Lou. Perhaps he had moved someone who could not take the dog with them. How else would he have acquired her? We never asked. Lindy Lou was a big, black chow with a black tongue and deep ruff of black fur round her neck. Chows were known to be fearsome and to look fearsome, yet she was the gentlest dog you could imagine.

Lindy Lou with Elizabeth

It was Father's job to groom her with a stiff brush and a steel comb and, as he combed her, her fur came out in handsful. He would sit on a stool in the kitchen with Lindy Lou sitting between his legs enjoying all the attention. It was my job to take her a walk, or rather for her to take me a walk. She was a strong dog and did not like going for walks. She was terrified of traffic. She would strain at the lead, pulling very hard and keeping in as close to the hedge as possible, gasping away as though the lead was choking her. She would set off as fast as possible, dragging me at the end of the lead, flying to keep up with her.

Out for a walk

I would often go up the road and past the house where I knew "orange bike" lived in the hope of seeing him but we would always be well away before there was any chance of seeing him as Lindy Lou had one object in mind: to get home as soon as possible. She would occasionally accompany us onto the front drive and sit close to the garage doors watching the people who passed as they cast a wary glance in her direction in case she moved. It was the dustmen who were terrified of her and would not come anywhere near the house until I had removed her. Had they known it, she was more frightened of them than they of her. I wonder what had terrified her so much at her previous home.

She lived with us for several years until one evening, as we were about to set off for the theatre, Mother called her in from the garden before locking the back door. Father was not with us as he was late returning from his day's work. Lindy Lou did not come in. Mother went to look for her but Lindy Lou had found her eternal resting place beneath the large rhododendron bush, half-way down the garden. Mother took something down to cover over her and left a note on the kitchen table for Father to find when he came home. Poor Father did what was necessary.

CHAPTER XXIV
Friends Up North

A little of Mother's history would now seem appropriate to continue my story. She was Ellen, generally known as Nell and, in her teens, went on holiday with a couple of friends. They met and enjoyed the company of a group of lads from up North, one being John Clegg who lived in Rochdale. He seemed very fond of Nell and they continued to correspond after returning home. Nell was invited up to Rochdale to meet his mother and two sisters, Amy, the younger, and Nellie – yes, another of the same name – the older sister. Mother and Nellie got on very well together and I suspect the sisters were hopeful of a closer association. But Mother had an admirer back home in Birmingham, another John, and in due course John in Birmingham and Nell became my mother and father. Correspondence and friendship continued between the friends up North, and Nellie Clegg and her husband Wilfred were invited to be my godparents, so now, as I grew up, I too became involved with the family up North.

Father did not have a car. Before the war he rode a motorbike, so when he wanted to take us on holiday, he borrowed his younger, bachelor brother's car. I remember a wonderful holiday in Devon, at Coombe Martin, when I was six and Elizabeth was two, a month or two before the war started. We played on the sands and in the rock pools where Elizabeth was safe, and improving after her operations. After this Father acquired a car but the war and petrol rationing soon put a stop to gallivanting around, not to be resumed until the war was over and petrol rationing eased.

Mother expressed a desire to go up North and renew the friendship with the Cleggs so Father agreed to drive us up one Sunday to Rochdale. And what a different experience it was for me after my country evacuation. Rochdale is a mill town where there were many cotton mills. Everything seemed dark grey and smoky from the many chimneys. The pavements were all dark grey brick blocks. Everything seemed dark grey and dismal.

John Clegg and his mother, to whom we gave the courtesy titles of "Uncle John" and "Grandma Clegg", lived in a small end-of-terrace house which was seen from the main road through the gap between two end-of-terrace houses, and could only be approached by a bridge over a brook. In subsequent years when we visited, Elizabeth and I would be excitedly looking out for this gap and the first sight of Grandma Clegg's house, hoping they would be in their doorway looking out for us as they had been previously informed by letter of the expected time of our arrival. Oh, a car could get to it by a roundabout way at the back of the terraced houses but we parked opposite the gap on the main road which saw very little traffic at that time.

I remember Mother offering us a comb as we drew nearer to our destination and saying "Comb your hair girls, make yourselves look smart." as she wanted us to make a good impression. We were made so very welcome.

The house had just one living room and a kitchen-cum-scullery downstairs and two bedrooms upstairs. Behind it was a steep bank, very close to the row of terraced houses and on top of that was a railway line. It seemed to have only goods trains running up there and I was very excited when one came rumbling along. Outside, at the front, over rough ground was the row of toilets and, if one needed to use the appointed one, a key had to be taken from the hook just inside the scullery door.

A little way away from this end-of-terrace house in a dark grey area of ground which passed as a play area was a solitary piece of play equipment which Elizabeth and I longed to go down to. It was a gigantic slide and chute, much bigger than we had ever seen before, with so many steps up to a great height, so it seemed to us, and a long, long slide down the other side. We were allowed to go for a short while and were told to be very careful. How we enjoyed running from the bottom of the chute to the bottom of the steps to climb up as fast as we could before the fast descent on the chute again. There was no-one else in the playground but us. When we came back, Grandma Clegg had laid a special tea for us, a special Sunday tea with meat on our tea plates and soft bap-like bread. A plate with a cake on it was special too.

It was at a time when people were putting on weight and were desirous of losing their excess poundage. There were no Slimming World or Weight Watchers' classes then but there were proprietary dietary foods to be bought in the shops. It was suggested that a satisfying meal of two special biscuits which included all the vitamins needed, followed by a glass of milk, taken twice a day, would help reduce weight. Grandma Clegg was taken with the idea and I remember one visit when, after we had all, including Grandma Clegg, finished our enjoyable tea, she took her two dietary biscuits and a glass of milk to help her lose weight!

After tea Uncle John, who worked in a cotton mill, showed us some of the raw cotton they used. His sister, Amy, lived a short distance away down the main road at Shawforth and by now had two sons, Peter and Freddie, and on the way home, we called in to see them. His sister Nellie and her husband, Wilfred, and their son, John, lived on The Wirral in Cheshire where they had a sweet shop, so to see them we had to make another Sunday visit at a later time.

Auntie Amy's Freddie had asthma, not helped by all the smoke and grime in the northern air and, after one visit we made up there to see them, we brought Freddie back with us for a holiday in Birmingham. He had an asthma attack, a bad one, but Mother coped, having been told what to expect and how to deal with it, but it was painful to witness and I for one was pleased when we went back up north to take him home. They must have been pleased with Mother's offer to have him for soon afterwards Uncle John made for both Elizabeth and me a pair of genuine clogs, black leather, with steel rims underfoot, which clattered whenever and wherever we walked in them. It was the sound heard everywhere in Rochdale as all the men and women wore clogs on their way to and from the mills.

Baby Jane had arrived at the time I was working towards my school certificate (now called GCSE) exams, and I had lots of homework to do and plenty of revision I was supposed to do! My bike rides to school were often accompanied by my boy friend, 'orange bike', now known as John (yet another John!), as he had

139

now left school and was working for his father in his office which was in a large house on the main road near to school. Whenever I passed the house I would glance at the windows to see if I could see him but I never did. It seemed he saw me riding my bike up the hill returning to afternoon school but I never knew.

The exams came and went and ahead were six weeks of glorious holiday, and this is when Auntie Amy invited me to go up to Shawforth and spend a holiday with her. By now, she had four sons, Peter, my age, Freddie, Elizabeth's age, Ian and Wilfred. Four boys were forever hungry so, on the back of her kitchen door, she hung a bag, a large bag, into which she popped all the crusts from the loaves of bread. Whenever a hungry boy entered the house he could assuage his hunger by helping himself to a crust. She also had a small greengrocer's shop. Her house was a much newer one and opposite to it rose the moor. I accepted the invitation and Father drove us up one Sunday in August. It was the first time since evacuation that I had been away from the family. Auntie Amy encouraged me to go with her to the shop where she was delighted to introduce her young visitor to all her customers. She encouraged me to serve the customers, which I did very hesitantly in case I gave the wrong weight or the wrong change. It was such a responsibility! Perhaps she thought shop work might be in my line when I left school. Peter, her son, had begun work in a coach firm. I was of an age to leave school and start work but that was not my idea at all. I was not ready to leave school yet!

I was drawn to the moor opposite the house. During this August the weather was fine and sunny and the outdoors and fresh air beckoned me. What a wonderful feeling I would have sitting up there on 'the tops' with superb views all round. I would take a book and sit up there in my Heaven, revisiting my countryside experience of a few years before, on the moor. The wild flowers and the birds were all around up there for my delight. The boys had bikes, boys' bikes with a cross bar, but that was no bar to me riding one and I asked if I could borrow one and go for a ride. There was hardly any traffic around. On one Sunday Peter said he would take me for a bike ride so we rode companionably to Todmorden, quite a way away. One evening Uncle John said he would take me a walk through the wood where Mother had walked when she was on holiday there. It was a very enjoyable evening, and once I looked at Uncle John and a thought crossed my mind; did he wonder how it would have been if I had been his daughter? He had never married.

My school certificate exam results were out and Father immediately sent me a congratulatory telegram. Seven credits and two passes. I was delighted with my success. Auntie Amy was delighted to hear of my success too and asked me to stay another week, which my parents were agreeable to, but John, my boyfriend, (oh dear, all these 'Johns), was not. He went to our house to ask if I had had my results and to know what they were, and to know when I was returning home. He was most put out to find that I was staying in Rochdale for another week. The next Sunday my parents, with Elizabeth, came to fetch me home and on arriving back quite late I said I would just take Lindy Lou out for a run as she had been indoors all day and I would pop up the road (for John lived in a house in the cul-de-sac just off the top end of our road) to let him know I was home. But he knew already because he had been watching from his bedroom window for our car to turn into our road. He had waited for hours! His idea was that I should leave school, as I was already (just) sixteen, and start work in an office! Indeed! That he should make such a suggestion! I was not ready to leave school yet. Was I not born to teach? I had already had plenty of practice with Elizabeth as my willing, and sometimes unwilling, pupil. No, an office was definitely not the direction in which I was heading. Ahead my path lay in a very different direction.

As to our friends up north, in later years sadness hit the family. The two younger boys, Ian and Wilfred, left to emigrate to Australia and Grandma Clegg died of breast cancer. We did make a journey up there for Mother to visit her in hospital but I did not accompany her. Auntie Amy was found on the kitchen floor behind the back door after suffering a heart attack and Uncle John refused to allow us to visit him after his face had suffered burns following a fire at the mill where he worked. Peter, Auntie Amy's eldest son, who was my age, did pay us a short visit as he was stationed at Lichfield during the first days of his National Service which all eighteen-year-old young men had to do when the war finished. Conscription only lasted a few years after the war ended.

CHAPTER XXV
Finale

Father's vans had been called into use many times for jobs other than removals. In the war years he had worked for the Ministry of Aviation transporting aircraft parts. In peacetime he was now more often moving pianos. He had previously provided transport for Sunday School outings and now he had a request to take Scouts and their equipment for their annual camping holiday. The destination was Oxwich Bay in South Wales. As mentioned before, I always asked if I could accompany Father on his journeys. On the appointed day the van was loaded with the busy help of all the Scouts, the Scout Leaders directing all activity and, eventually, the stacks of equipment and provisions disappeared from outside to inside the van, along with all participating bodies, who found something to sit on from where they could watch the outside world from the back of the van as the journey progressed. The van had a drop back which came half way up the van and was pegged in place so that the top half was open to the elements.

They were a merry crowd, singing as they travelled along. When we drew nearer to the site Father stopped to ask the Scout Leader exactly where he was going but the Scout Leader was not quite sure! Out came the maps which were studied to pinpoint the spot and for Father to work out the approach, which was down a narrow lane with overhanging trees. Now Father was careful with his vans and approached slowly as the branches scratched the top of the van. He was somewhat bothered. However, the field was reached, the contents, alive and otherwise, removed from the van and all made ready for our return.

The Scout camp was on site for a week and the time came round for Father to return again to Oxwich Bay to complete his booking and bring the Scouts back home again. This time John, my boyfriend, asked if he could come along too – quite a different experience for him. On his way down the week before Father had noted a particularly large branch which overhung the lane and had decided to do something about it. We stopped. Father climbed into the back of the van and unhooked a ladder, then jumped down with a saw in his hand. He had stacked it away out of sight. "Right, Ann, you hold the ladder this side; John, you hold the ladder the other side and I'll rest it on this branch." He climbed up a few rungs of the ladder and began to saw off the branch. One's imagination soars as he saws! A proper Laurel and Hardy scene! What a laugh we had.

The Tree Cutter

Job done satisfactorily without mishap. The branch would no longer be there to scratch the top of the van. We proceeded to the Scout camp. While everything was being loaded John and I managed to get down to the sea through all the wet vegetation. There had been so much rain. We were soaked from feet up to knees but we had seen the sea.

Around this time Uncle Howard involved Father in a project that had been much on his mind. Possibly they had been discussing it, whilst talking 'man business' beside the fire in the lounge. Uncle Howard wanted to build a caravan and, as a pattern maker with his own workshop it was well within his capabilities. At this time, at the end of the war, there were very few caravans to be seen. Commercial manufacturers were few. There were no caravan showrooms and no caravan sites. Uncle Howard had one problem. He had no space where he could build his caravan and this is where he sought Father's help.

144

At the yard beside my grandparents' house at number 2, Cowper Street, there were not just two giant gates which rolled open to allow vans to enter the yard, there were three, for at the further, left-hand side at the front, the third gate rolled along to reveal a covered garage hidden behind. It was in here that the smallest van was often garaged and where Father parked a van whenever he was servicing it. Uncle Howard wondered if he could have the use of this garage to build his caravan. They must have come to some mutual agreement though Grandfather was not enthusiastic over the idea. As Father had originally been at the technical college he was also able to help in the construction. It soon began to take shape in the covered garage. Every spare minute was spent in the making of this caravan. Whenever I went to Grandmother's I would pop my head round the door to see how it was progressing and I remember once being told to keep away from the work as they were fitting sheets of fibreglass for insulation between the wooden interior and the outer bodywork. It was certainly growing apace.

Auntie Miriam would be making the curtains and the covers for the seats which would serve as the beds. She was making cushions for comfort and when all else had been bought to fit out the caravan it was finally ready for inspection. It was a superb piece of craftsmanship.

The next step was to find a site for it to be parked for its first holiday occupants, Uncle Howard, Auntie Miriam and Carol of course. Then when the site was found and booked the caravan had to be transported there. Neither Uncle's nor Father's cars were big enough or powerful enough to tow it. How about using the smallest of the furniture vans? It seemed an excellent idea. So the furniture removal van was taken to have a tow bar fitted. The van tow bar was, of necessity, longer than a car tow bar but was correctly balanced. And so came the day for the journey.

The destination was a farm at Ridge Road, near to Maidencombe in Devon, not far from Torquay. A furniture removal van towing a large caravan was not a common sight and caught the interest of all whom they passed, including the Police. They were followed, overtaken and flagged down to stop. Now what! Everything was in order as far as Father knew. The Police approached and began to ask questions as to the weight distribution and suitability of a van towing a caravan. Being satisfied with Father's answers they then took out a tape measure and began taking measurements of tow bar and distances between van and caravan. They asked about the weight and strength and anything else they could think of. Eventually they could find nothing wrong and Father and Uncle were given clearance to continue their journey. Ridge Road was reached and, after visiting the farmer, the caravan was pitched for its first holiday.

Uncle's caravan at Ridge Road

We also enjoyed our first holiday in Uncle Howard's caravan, at the end of which I had something extra to look forward to. While I was away with my family in Devon, John, my boyfriend, was away with his parents in Scotland. He saw a way to enjoy his greatest hobby and planned his journey home by train from Scotland via Devon! He came to Torquay where he arrived from his overnight experience early in the morning. It was arranged that I would walk from Ridge Road along the main road to Torquay and meet him on the way. I did not have to walk far when I saw him striding out up the hill. Back at Ridge Road a room in the farmhouse had been booked for him to freshen up and stay the night before he took me back to Torquay where we caught the steam train the next day back to Birmingham. He was particularly keen to travel the coast line through Dawlish and was keen too to point out to me all the places of interest on our memorable journey home. It was the perfect way to end my holiday.

Ann and John at Oxwich Bay

A new era was now about to begin for, while John was leaving Birmingham to embark on his National Service, I would be returning to school.

Acknowledgements

Without the help of my sister, Jane, this book would never have come to fruition. I owe her all my thanks for the preparation, her time spent on putting it on her computer and arranging all the photographs in the appropriate places.

My sincere thanks and appreciation go to Jane MacIntosh for the time she has given checking over, giving advice and editing my story.

Thanks to Ann Wallace for her time so generously given in attention to photographs and her assistance in publishing this book

Ann lives with her husband in Devon. From where they now live they can see the coastal railway line running beside the cliffs in Dawlish. Ann is a walks leader with the local 'Walking for Health' group. Her hobbies include needle crafts, gardening, reading and writing to friends both at home and abroad.

36714671R00085

Printed in Poland
by Amazon Fulfillment
Poland Sp. z o.o., Wrocław